NATURA
HEALTHY
DOGS

Dr. Carol Osborne

MARSHALL PUBLISHING • LONDON

A Marshall Edition
Conceived, edited and designed by
Marshall Editions Ltd
The Orangery
161 New Bond Street
London W1Y 9PA

First published in the UK in 1999 by
Marshall Publishing Ltd

ISBN: 1 84028 288 6

Originated in Singapore by Pica
Printed and bound in China by Excel

Project Editor Conor Kilgallon

Art Editor Patrick Carpenter

Consultant David Alderton

Managing Editor Clare Currie

Designer Sue Storey

Indexer Jill Dormon

Picture Research Antonella Mauro

Editorial Director Ellen Dupont

Art Director Dave Goodman

Editorial Coordinator Ros Highstead

Production Nikki Ingram

Note

Every effort has been taken to ensure that
all information in this book is correct and
compatible with national standards generally
accepted at the time of publication. This book
is not intended to replace consultation with your
veterinarian or alternative therapy practitioner.
The author and publisher disclaim any liability,
loss, injury or damage incurred as a consequence,
directly or indirectly, of the use and application
of the contents of this book.

CONTENTS

The Head

The Digestive System

Skin and Hair

Systemic Illnesses

Behavioural Problems

First Aid

INTRODUCTION

There has been a revolution in veterinary health care. Dogs now live well into their late teens because of improvements in sanitation and treatment of infectious disease. Veterinary medicine has made great advances in treating chronic conditions such as heart, kidney and liver disease. In addition we have learned that prevention and early detection of disease along with proper nutrition are cornerstones to good health. Increasingly, research has shown that an evaluation of internal and external environmental factors are paramount to restore balance, health, and harmony for all of us.

No one form of medicine has all the answers; if it did, the rest would disappear. It doesn't matter if a therapy is old or new, eastern or western. What does matter is whether it cures the condition. It is a common misconception that holistic and homeopathic medicine are synonymous, but they are not. Holistic is also known as alternative medicine and deals with the whole patient using a range of therapies: herbalism, homeopathy, acupuncture, chiropractic, flower essences and naturopathy. It is not meant to replace conventional veterinary medicine but, used in conjunction with it, offers your pet the best of both worlds. By the convergence of conventional and alternative practices, complementary medicine is enhancing all of life on earth.

USING THE FACT FILE

This book is divided into six chapters: 1. The Head; 2. The Digestive System; 3. Skin and Hair; 4. Systemic Illnesses; 5. Behavioural Problems; 6. First Aid. If you know which subject you wish to look up, then simply turn to the relevant tab, the colour-coded subject dividers. On each, you will find a table of contents for that part of the book. If you are unsure where to find the information you need, turn to the alphabetical index on page 112.

TEXT AND ILLUSTRATIONS

Drawings of your dog's anatomy and photography illustrating alternative treatments can be found throughout the book. The text is clearly divided into a description of the problem, its causes and what a vet, or you, can do to help.

USE WITH CARE

This book is not intended to provide veterinary advice or to be used as a substitute for advice from your vet. It is important to consult with your vet before your dog begins any therapy, whether or not it is included in this book.

CHOOSING A VET

When you decide on a vet, your initial reaction is generally your best guide. You need to find a person with whom you feel confident and comfortable and one who is conveniently located. It is advisable to register with a vet soon after acquiring your dog, so that you can arrange for your new pet to have a health check and receive any outstanding vaccinations.

To help you with your choice you can first check the vet's credentials. Ask for references and if possible pay the practice a visit. Second, make sure that the vet can offer all the services you may need: boarding, grooming, hospitalization and 24-hour emergency care. It does help to register close to home, in case of an emergency, and you may also need to take the practice's opening hours into account if you are working. Most veterinary practices have an appointment system.

Another factor that may influence your decision is whether you will see the same vet all each time you visit. This obviously has the benefit of continuity, particularly if your dog needs a lengthy spell of treatment. On the other hand, a larger practice will have a greater number of vets available for consultation and much more scope for specialization—such as alternative medicine—which is an advantage. You should make your vet your partner to provide optimal health care throughout your dog's life.

On page 111 you will find a list of organizations that can refer you to complementary veterinary medical practitioners. Alternatively, you can search the Internet to locate information you may need.

HOW DO I GET THE BEST FROM MY VET?

Work together with your dog's vet as a partner in your pet's health team. When your dog is sick, jot down the most important factors of its medical condition. These should include:

• Your dog's age and history.

• The signs of the illness, including when they first appeared and how long they have been going on.

• Any medications that your dog may be currently taking.

HOLISTIC MEDICINE

Research has shown that health is influenced by physical, mental, and emotional factors. Holistic medicine includes an evaluation of diet, emotions, and lifestyle, as well as a physical examination. It is an approach that deals with the whole patient—so in the case of your pet there may be a range of complementary therapies that will be employed to find the best treatment. This book tells you about some complementary treatments, notably herbal remedies and homeopathy, which will often help to alleviate the symptoms of illness and make your pet more comfortable. Do remember that if you are worried about your dog's health you should always contact your vet.

HERBALISM

Using plants and herbs for medicinal purposes is an ancient practice. You can cut up fresh herbs and mix them into the food, or use the liquid "tincture" form, which is the most potent and the best choice in most cases. Herbs can be used externally as dips and tonics for skin problems. They also have unique properties when it comes to stimulating the immune system for diseases that are untreatable by conventional methods. It is advisable to consult an experienced herbal practitioner for recommended dosages and protocols, since most are not yet formalized.

HOMEOPATHY

Homeopathists believe that administering an extremely dilute form of a substance similar to the one causing the symptoms stimulates the body to overcome the illness itself. The remedies used are all natural and are derived from plants, minerals, or animal products. They are precisely diluted, one part to 90 parts alcohol, then vigorously shaken to become activated. The more dilute the remedy, the stronger it gets and the more intrinsic energy it releases. This energy rebalances the body's "vital force" or "chi", which stimulates the body's immune system to heal itself.

You can buy most homeopathic remedies in a specific strength—the number after the name indicates the strength. If you have any doubts or need guidance, seek the advice of your homeopathic pharmacist or vet. The remedies can be given as pellets or crushed to powder and given by mouth. They must be handled and given according to specific guidelines or they can become inactivated.

Homeopathy remedies are compatible with nutritional and chiropractic therapies. However, they should not be used with acupuncture or strong herbal tinctures because they can inactivate each other. Working with a homeopathic vet is essential for successful therapy.

OTHER TREATMENTS

A number of other complementary approaches are useful with dogs. Always seek treatment from skilled practitioners in the field of alternative veterinary medicine.

FLOWER ESSENCES

Flower essences are diluted flower preparations that are used to treat behavioural problems, fears, and other psychological problems, especially those associated with stress. They help to rebalance mental and emotional well-being. Originally, Edward Bach, a British physician in the 1930s, developed 38 different flower essences, each of which was used to rebalance a different emotional situation. These essences are therefore also called bach flower remedies.

Rescue Remedy is one of the most popular. It is a mixture of five flower essences and is commonly used after a physical or emotional trauma or during a stressful situation. For example, for a dog stressed by the introduction of a new pet into the home, you can place three drops in or on the mouth or tongue two or three times daily.

ACUPUNCTURE

Acupuncture is the insertion of needles into specific body points to stimulate the body's immune system to heal itself. It is used to help dogs with hip dysplasia, arthritis, and bowel diseases with intractible vomiting and diarrhoea as well as epilepsy. The relief is generally temporary and eight or more treatments are often needed for positive results.

CHIROPRACTIC

Chiropractic is the manipulation of the spinal cord to adjust misplaced vertebrae that may be damaging nerves and impeding movement. It may be useful to relieve musculoskeletal pain resulting from trauma, arthritis or other degenerative processes.

NATUROPATHY

Naturopaths believe that diseases are caused by a build-up of toxins in the body. They recommend a regime of good nutrition and exercise combined with bathing, massage, and sunshine.

GLANDULAR THERAPY

These are biologically active nutritional supplements given as treats or mixed with food. Many contain glands from hormone secreting organs, such as the thyroid, and are used to stimulate a weakened gland to function normally.

1

THE HEAD

Signs of an illness are often seen first in the facial area. Watch out for eye discharges and runny noses, which can be clues to something going wrong. Changes in appetite and behaviour are also early indicators of a problem. Many infectious diseases are easily transmitted in the air by coughing and sneezing as well as by dog-to-dog contact, through shared food and water bowls, as well as faeces, vomit and contaminated items the dog comes across. You should remember that puppies lack natural immunity and this makes them extremely susceptible to diseases. As a new owner of a puppy or even an older dog, make an appointment to see your vet within 48 hours.

CONJUNCTIVITIS

Your dog's eyes should normally be clear, bright, and free of discharge. Red eyes in a dog can signal problems requiring treatment that ranges from eye drops to emergency surgery. The leading cause of eye disease in dogs is conjunctivitis, inflammation of the membranes lining the inside of the eyelids. It leads to red, swollen, itchy, watery eyes. All owners should recognize the signs of an eye problem or injury and get treatment as soon as possible, so the damage does not get any worse.

SYMPTOMS

- Redness and inflammation around the eyes.
- Mucus-like or watery discharge.
- Itchiness.
- Excessive blinking.
- Excessive tear production.

CAUSES

- Allergies to airborne pollens and moulds are the major cause of conjunctivitis.

- Bacterial infections are often associated with thick yellow or greenish discharge.

- Genetic conditions can be a cause of eye problems. These include entropion, where the lids are turned inward, or ectropion, where the lower eyelids droop down. In entropion, an excessive amount of eyelid tissue drags across the surface of the eye, causing irritation that can lead to ulceration. This becomes apparent in young dogs by the age of six months. Ectropion is less serious, and is evident in breeds such as the bloodhound. It results in the exposure of the reddish mucous membrane, which is normally concealed under the lower eyelid. This delicate exposed tissue can become inflamed by dirt or dust, or even affected by strong wind.

Dogs with large eyelids, such as the chow, can suffer from entropion.

• Distichiasis is an inherited condition caused by the presence of another row of eyelashes, and is especially common in some smaller breeds, such as the cocker spaniel and Pekingese. The extra eyelashes rub across the surface of the eye and cause variable degrees of irritation, depending on which part of the eye's surface they touch. Surgery is generally the only long-term solution to such genetic conditions.

• Foreign material—such as bristly bits of grasses and weeds—can get lodged in the eyes of hunting and outdoor dogs, especially those with ectropion.

• Dogs with cataracts and distemper virus can also get conjunctivitis.

• Since there are so many causes of eye problems, if they recur it's important to ask the vet to diagnose and eliminate the cause. Keep the eyes clean and apply appropriate medication.

Warning

Never allow your dog to put its head out of the window of a moving car. Not only is it dangerous, it also increases the chance of your pet getting conjunctivitis.
    Conjunctivitis is far more likely to occur if particles of dirt are forced into the dog's eyes by the rushing wind from a car window. This creates irritation and then inflammation sets in which can cause a great deal of misery.

Smaller breeds, such as the Pekingese, can inherit distichiasis, or extra eyelashes that irritate the surface of the eye.

COMPLEMENTARY TREATMENTS

⊠ HERBAL REMEDIES

For red, itchy eyes, use raspberry leaf tea as an eyewash, or put a drop of cod liver oil in the affected eye three to four times a day. Raw cucumber juice, applied in two to three drops three to four times a day, can help soothe irritations and allergies.

CORNEAL ULCERS

A corneal ulcer is an abrasion to the top layer of skin lining the cornea. It is the third most common eye problem in dogs and has many causes. These include scratches and superficial abrasions, and foreign objects like grass seeds and weeds that can lodge behind the third eyelid and cause injury. Rough play between new pets in the home (puppies and kittens) can also accidentally injure the cornea. Occasionally, bathing and grooming can result in an ulcer—it is a good idea to apply an eye lubricant before bathing and grooming to protect the eyes from shampoo and hair. Genetic conditions such as eyelashes turning inward (trichiasis) and eyelids that roll in (entropion) also create corneal trauma. Certain breeds suffer more than others. Breeds with pushed-in noses have big round eyes and cannot blink very well. These breeds tend to get dried-out eyes which are prone to ulcers. Common signs of an ulcer include squinting, watering, excess tears, and redness or swelling of the eyes. Initially ulcers are very painful because the eye contains more nerves than any other body part relative to its size.

WHAT YOUR VET CAN DO

• The vet will use a dye to stain the eye; it causes the ulcerated corneal tissue to turn a greenish colour. With proper treatment, most ulcers heal in three to five days. Medication generally consists of a topical lubricant and a topical antibiotic to prevent a bacterial infection. The ulcer may be restained a few days later to ensure it is healed. When ulcers do not heal promptly referral to a veterinary eye specialist is necessary to prevent corneal perforation.

COMPLEMENTARY TREATMENTS

🖵 HOMEOPATHIC REMEDIES

To relieve pain and inflammation of the eyes, *Aconitum napellus* 30c (monkshood) may be helpful. Give the dog two whole or three crushed pellets. Allow no food for one hour before or one hour after the treatment. Do not repeat the treatment for a full month, then reassess the dog's condition.

CATARACTS

Cataracts are extremely prevalent in dogs. A normal lens, which sits behind the pupil, is transparent and focuses incoming light on to the retina which then sends the image to the brain where vision is perceived. When the cells and protein of the lens begin to deteriorate a cataract forms. The lens gets cloudy and light cannot be transmitted to the retina, so vision is impaired.

EYE STRUCTURE

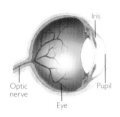

Iris

Optic nerve

Pupil

Eye

CAUSES

- Inflammation of the eye due to trauma or infectious agents.
- Diseases (i.e. diabetes).
- "Geriatric" cataracts are part of ageing.
- "Juvenile" cataracts are breed related, appearing at a young age (for example in cocker spaniels, all poodles, and Siberian husky).

SYMPTOMS

Change in colour of one or both eyes: milky white or blue-grey.

Warning

Juvenile cataracts happen at an early age. There are dissolving types (with cortisone drops the lens clears and vision is restored) and non-dissolving types (total irreversible lens damage). Juvenile cataracts are genetic in certain pure-breds. Responsible breeders have their dogs checked by a veterinary ophthalmologist.

WHAT YOUR VET CAN DO

- The sooner cataract surgery is done, the better the chance of restoring your dog's vision. The procedure, called phacoemulsification, involves a machine that emits high-frequency sound waves that destroy the lens. A suction device then removes the lens particles from the eye. An artificial lens, called an intraocular lens implant (IOL) replaces the old lens. The success rate is over 90 percent and vision is quickly restored.

- The vet will want to assess the eyes before deciding on surgery. This is done with an electroretinogram (ERG). Any hereditary eye problems, like progressive retinal atrophy (PRA), will also need to be ruled out.

COMPLEMENTARY TREATMENTS

▢ HOMEOPATHIC REMEDIES

Conium maculatum 6c (poison hemlock) taken once daily (one pellet) for a month can be especially helpful when a cataract is due to injury. Either Silicea 30c or Phosphorus 30c work better in advanced cases. Give a tablet twice daily over the course of three days and then restrict the dosage to a single tablet given twice a week.

CHERRY EYE AND DRY EYE

Throughout their lives some dogs can be prone to particular eye conditions. Cherry eye is defined as prolapse of the gland of the third eyelid. The medical term is glandular hypertrophy. Dry eye describes changes that occur in the eye resulting from a lack of tears. Vets call this "KCS", which stands for keratoconjunctivitis sicca.

CHERRY EYE

• In addition to the upper and lower eyelids, dogs (and cats) have a third eyelid that originates at the inside corner of the eye (closest to the nose). This third eyelid acts like a windshield wiper and helps protect the eye. In addition, it contains a gland that produces 30 percent of the tear film which keeps the clear front part of the eye, the cornea, well lubricated. Cherry eye results when this gland goes wrong.

• The exact cause of cherry eye is somewhat controversial. Some experts say it is a genetic condition because cocker spaniels, beagles, bulldogs and Pekingese seem to be predisposed. But other breeds including bloodhounds, great Danes and basset hounds are also commonly affected. Whether or not trauma is also a cause is still a matter of debate between veterinary ophthalmologists.

• In dogs with cherry eye the gland is red and fleshy. It looks like a small cherry that suddenly pops up and protrudes from the corner of the eye. The other eye may or may not also be affected at a later date. Dogs with cherry eye are usually under a year old. In addition to the redness and swelling, a clear or mucus-like discharge may also occur.

• Surgical treatment is usually done to replace the gland back inside the third eyelid. That way the gland continues to produce "tears" and the risk of dry eye is therefore prevented. The prognosis for such cases is excellent.

• Other treatments include surgical removal of the gland which often leads to a lack of tear film production and can result in dry eye. Ignoring the cherry eye is another option. Sometimes it goes away on its own in two to three weeks, at other times it leads to further eye disease. You should discuss treatment options, which will vary depending on the breed, with your vet.

DRY EYE

• Tears are essential to keep the cornea healthy, supplying it with oxygen and food. If there is a lack of tear film production, destructive changes occur quickly, leading to dry eye. This causes the cornea to become pigmented, scarred, and ulcerated. Partial vision loss (even blindness) can result. The eyes of dogs with KCS sting all the time, just like yours do on a windy day. The condition is diagnosed by a test that measures the number of tears the eye produces in one minute.

• There are several situations that can cause dry eye. These include hypothyroidism (see p. 69); tear gland infections caused by the canine distemper virus (see p. 22), or immune system diseases (such as cancer).

• The ususal treatments are topical antibiotics and anti-inflammatory (cortisone) drugs which treat secondary bacterial infections of the eye and reduce corneal inflammation. Artificial tear ointment helps lubricate the dry cornea. A range of different drugs may be prescribed to relieve symptoms and cause or stimulate an increase in actual tear production.

• If medication doesn't work, your vet may consider a surgical procedure called a parotid duct transposition (PDT).

• The prognosis for dry eye is good with consistent therapy. If a dog isn't treated, it may suffer recurrent corneal ulcers, bacterial infections, and even become blind.

COMPLEMENTARY TREATMENTS

☐ HOMEOPATHIC REMEDIES

It is possible that *Zincum metallicum* 30c, given twice daily, may assist in cases of dry eye, especially when the treatment is used in conjunction with artificial tear fluid.

DENTAL CARE

Puppies have no teeth at birth. They start to appear after about a month when the young dog begins to eat solid food. Altogether, there are 28 of these "deciduous", or "milk", teeth, which are replaced by a permanent set by the time the dog is between four and six months old. The teething period can be very uncomfortable for the dog, and can cause it to become destructive around the house. During this time you will need to distract your dog's attention away from the furniture and your shoes by giving it a selection of toys to chew.

Adult dogs have 42 teeth, the most prominent being the four large canines at the front. Once the dog's permanent teeth have grown, there will be no further replacements, even if teeth are lost through damage or disease. They need to keep them for good health.

WHAT YOU CAN DO

• Good dental care is important. In dogs, just as in people, bacteria combine with saliva and food particles to form plaque. It accumulates in the spaces between the teeth and gums, and combines with calcium salts to form tartar, or calculus as it is also called. The bacteria, plaque, and tartar irritate and inflame the gums, causing gingivitis.

• Be extra careful if you have a small breed. They are more prone to dental disease than larger breeds because their teeth are often too large for the size of their mouth. This causes crowding, which leads to rapid accumulation of destructive bacteria and plaque.

• To prevent dental problems, regular brushing of your dog's teeth is vital, right from the puppy stage. Brush the outer surface of the teeth for 30 seconds with a toothpaste made for dogs. For fussy dogs, try beef broth or chicken soup on the brush.

• Commercially available diets can help prevent bad breath and inflammation of the gums and mouth. Another option is to feed a homemade diet. Give proportions of 20 percent meat and eggs, 60 percent fresh cooked vegetables, and 20 percent fresh chopped greens.

Check your dog's teeth and gums regularly for signs of gingivitis and other dental problems.

A DOG'S TEETH

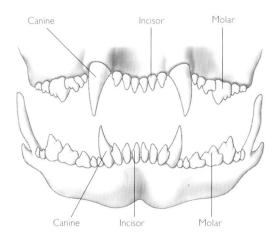

Canine   Incisor   Molar

Canine   Incisor   Molar

WHAT YOUR VET CAN DO

• Professional dental cleaning involves the use of an ultrasonic machine that vibrates the calculus off the surface of the teeth. Calculus from under the gum tissue is carefully removed using a hand scaler. After this the teeth are polished and a fluoride treatment is applied for protection.

• Your vet can also give the dog a dental examination, remove loose teeth, and treat tooth abscesses which occur when pus builds up.

COMPLEMENTARY TREATMENTS

⊠ HERBAL REMEDIES
Special brushing kits, consisting of a tooth brush and an oil-based sage toothpaste, are available for dogs.

Raw carrots also act as a natural toothbrush for your dog and will prevent a build-up of plaque on the dog's teeth.

After your dog has had any dental work, use goldenseal (*Hydrastis canadensis*) to help with the healing process. To make the solution, add 5 ml (1 tsp) of the powdered root stock to 600 ml (1 pint) of boiling water. Once this has cooled, you can wash out your dog's mouth with the clear part of the solution, sucking it up in a syringe (without a needle).

▢ HOMEOPATHIC REMEDIES
Fragaria 6c given three times a month can slow the accumulation of calculus.

Raw carrots help prevent the build-up of plaque.

DENTAL PROBLEMS

Disease of the mouth is the most common health problem treated in small animal clinics. At least 85 percent of all dogs and cats over two years old have periodontal disease, which left untreated is now known to be a leading cause of heart disease. Bacteria from the mouth also increase the risk of liver and kidney disease. The good news is that dental problems are both preventable and controllable.

SYMPTOMS

- Bad breath.
- Red swollen gums.
- Discoloured teeth.

SIGNS OF DENTAL PROBLEMS

- Breed, genetics, age, diet, and general health all contribute to the prevalence and severity of gum disease. If your dog is having trouble eating, changes its way of chewing, is reluctant to eat, or paws at its face, it might have a dental problem. Depression and lethargy can also result from infection in the mouth.

- If gingivitis is not treated, the bacteria grow in the spaces between the gum line and form pus, which eventually separates the tooth from the gum, as well as from the jawbone underneath. Once the jawbone is infected, the result is periodontal disease, which is irreversible. Dental cleaning and plaque control at this stage can prevent the periodontal disease from getting worse.

- If periodontal disease is left untreated, this allows bacteria to enter the bloodstream, spread to and cause disease in other organs including the heart, the liver, and the kidneys. Eventually the gums recede and the teeth fall out.

- Dogs rarely get cavities. When they do, it is more often at the root of the tooth rather than at the crown, and can lead to root abscesses (a build-up of pus from bacteria). Generally, tooth extractions are needed at this point. Some veterinary dental specialists offer root canals, caps, and braces for dogs.

COMPLEMENTARY TREATMENTS

HERBAL REMEDIES
Myrrh (*Commiphora myrrha*) may assist healing. Add 5 ml (1 tsp) of the resin to 600 ml (1 pint) of boiling water, allow to cool and then spray over the affected area using a syringe.

Rubbing oil from a vitamin E capsule on the gums once daily helps relieve inflammation.

Myrrh

CANCERS

Dogs suffer from a variety of cancers to the head, the mouth being a common site. Breeds with dark pigment, such as black cocker spaniels and chows, are prone to melanoma in the mouth. Signs include swelling around apparently normal teeth. Cancer of the nasal passages and sinus accounts for 2 percent of all cancer in dogs. It is not known whether sniffing chemicals and carcinogens such as herbicides and pesticides is a factor. Cocker spaniels with chronic ear infections occasionally develop carcinomas of the wax-producing glands.

The site of an injury may at some point develop into cancer.

Warning

A benign growth of the gum is known as an epulis. If it is left to grow very large it may trigger gum disease, since food deposits can become trapped in the gap between the tumour and the tooth, allowing bacteria to multiply and attack the gum.

WHAT YOU AND YOUR VET CAN DO

• Inspect your dog's mouth regularly, perhaps while brushing its teeth, so that you can spot problems early on. Any growth in the mouth is potentially serious and should be examined by a vet as soon as possible.

• High energy radiation therapy provides the longest survival time for nasal tumours. Dogs live for one to one and a half years more with this treatment but eventually die as a result of the tumour.

• Skin, nose, and mouth cancers can be prevented by limiting exposure to ultraviolet light. Keep your dog away from excessive sunlight.

COMPLEMENTARY TREATMENTS

◻HOMEOPATHIC REMEDIES

Two remedies that may help to lead to a regression of an epulis are often recommended, especially when surgery has already been tried. *Calcarea fluorica* 30c twice each week can be beneficial, while for young dogs, *Calcarea carbonica* 30c can be used.

EAR PROBLEMS

The inside lining of the ear is normally smooth with a small amount of wax build-up. However, many problems can cause the ears to be irritated, inflamed, and infected. Any of these causes left untreated can lead to more complicated problems, including inner-ear infections, hearing loss, haematomas (when blood vessels rupture in the ear flap causing a swollen area), and brain inflammation. Most dogs let you know their ears are uncomfortable by scratching, shaking, or tilting their heads. Breeds with long floppy ears and narrow ear canals are especially at risk, as well as dogs that are swimmers and those that live in warm, humid places. Vets often use terms like "cocker ear" and "swimmer's ear" to describe ear problems in these dogs.

CAUSES

• Ear mites are most common in cats and puppies. These microscopic mites have hairs on their body that irritate the animal's ears, causing itching and a dark brown coffee-like residue. Mites live their entire life in the ear and can be transferred to other pets in your home, so all your pets need treatment once mites are diagnosed.

SYMPTOMS

• Irritation.
• Unpleasant odour.
• Discharge.

• Allergic reactions to pollen, mould, plants and fleas are common in dogs. In addition to itching their ears, many dogs also lick their feet and rub their face. Ear infections associated with allergies often recur until the underlying cause of the allergy is determined.

• Yeasts normally live in the ear in small numbers. Large numbers cause a smelly, waxy build-up. Dark, deep ear canals with minimal air flow promote an ideal environment for yeasts to flourish.

• Bacteria often occur secondary to inflammation from any cause, and result in a painful smelly pus-type discharge.

• Trauma to the ear from plant seeds or over-aggressive cleaning can also cause pain and inflammation of the ears.

The vet uses an otoscope to check ears so the right treatment can be prescribed.

WHAT YOU AND YOUR VET CAN DO

• The vet will examine a sample of the ear discharge under a microscope to diagnose the cause of the problem, then choose the most effective treatment. It will usually be a composite remedy to kill ear mites and yeasts. The vet can also run allergy tests.

• Homemade ear cleaners are effective. Mix 5 ml (1 tsp) of Calendula with 2.5 ml (half tsp) of sea salt in 250 ml (8 fl oz) of water. Or mix equal quantities of white vinegar and water. Squirt the cleaner into each ear canal and massage for five to ten seconds. Use a cotton ball or piece of gauze to ease out the debris.

• The infection is cleared once the residue is gone, along with the odour and discomfort. After that, if you clean out your dog's ears once a week, it will help prevent recurrences and allow early detection of another problem. Never clean any deeper than you can see.

Long, floppy ears are poorly ventilated and are susceptible to infection and irritation.

Warning

If your dog continually scratches and shakes its head because of an ear infection, the blood vessels in the outer flap of its ear can be damaged. Blood leaks into the ear flap and causes a swollen ear (a condition known as a haematoma). Your vet will need to correct this surgically by draining out the blood. Tumours and polyps in the ears must also be dealt with by your vet. Surgical correction may often be necessary.

COMPLEMENTARY TREATMENTS

☐ HOMEOPATHIC REMEDIES

For recurrent severe inflammation or excess wax, use *Silicea* 30c: two whole or three crushed pellets every 12 hours for three treatments. Allow no food 30 minutes before or after treatment. Wait one month and then reassess the condition. For allergic, red, irritated ears try *Pulsatilla* 6c (windflower): one pellet every third day for 30 days. Allow no food 10 minutes before or after treatment. In chronic cases your vet may recomment *Tellurium* 30c. The usual dosage is one tablet twice daily for three days, and then a weekly dose until the inflammation has cleared up.

DISTEMPER

A highly infectious viral disease of dogs, canine distemper attacks the lungs, brain and spinal cord. It occurs worldwide wherever there are dogs, with a death rate of 80 percent in puppies and 50 percent in adults. The virus is airborne and also spreads between dogs by contact

with contaminated food and water bowls, as well as urine and faeces. Other animals including foxes and wolves also carry distemper. Vaccination is very effective, and is normally given to young puppies in a series of shots and then is backed up by annual boosters. You shouldn't let them lapse.

WHAT YOU AND YOUR VET CAN DO

• Immediate treatment is your dog's best chance for survival. Since no specific cure exists, supportive care is critical. The younger the dog, the greater the risk because the immune system is not fully developed at this stage of life.

• The vet will give intraveneous fluids at the vomiting and diarrhoea stage. Once vomiting stops, fluids are given by mouth. Try vegetable broth or honey water (a small spoon of honey in a cup of water).

• Gradually add in food, depending on the presence or not of diarrhoea. Offer a bland diet of puréed chicked in small amounts four to six times daily and continue supportive care as required for diarrhoea (see p. 30).

• The pads of the feet also become thickened as a result of this virus and develop cracks. This is why distemper is sometimes called "hard pad". The most serious symptoms, however, derive from the effect of the condition on the brain and result in the dog suffering from fits, including twitching of the eyes and head and champing of the jaws. The dog may collapse and become paralysed, with little hope of recovery.

SYMPTOMS

• At first the signs resemble a bad cold with a fever (temperature of 39.5–40.5°C).

• Runny eyes and nose with thick yellowish-green pus; later coughing, vomiting, diarrhoea and weight loss will develop.

• In the final stages the nervous system is attacked (this may take up to a month to become apparent); muscle twitching, paralysis, convulsions and death may result.

• In those dogs that do survive, muscle twitching may be permanent.

Warning

Behavioural changes later in life can be the result of a previous distemper infection. Loss of coordination and a high-stepping gait are common indicators, along with repetitive behaviour patterns, such as repeatedly pacing up and down. The precise cause is unclear, but degenerative changes in the brain linked with the distemper virus are often suspected.

• Those dogs that do recover from distemper may be afflicted by chorea, or an uncontrollable rhythmic twitching of muscles, often on the head.

• Puppies may be left with permanently scarred teeth as a result of distemper. Brown depressions indicate damage to the outer white coating of the enamel. They are also particularly prone to pustules on the abdomen, although these will clear with appropriate treatment.

Vaccination of young dogs is effective against distemper.

COMPLEMENTARY TREATMENTS

HERBAL REMEDIES

Use a herbal conjunctivitis solution: make from 150 ml (10 tbsp) of rosemary, 75 ml (5 tbsp) of thyme boiled in 1 litre (2 pints) of water for 15 minutes. When cool use to clean the eyes and nose several times a day. One to two drops of almond oil on your pet's eyelids and cracked nose is soothing.

HOMEOPATHIC REMEDIES

Distemperinum 30c taken as early as possible twice daily may be beneficial. Use Pulsatilla 6c for thick eye discharge. Give one pellet every four hours.

KENNEL COUGH

Canine kennel cough is a highly contagious airborne disease affecting the respiratory system of dogs. It is usually produced by a combination of bacterial and viral agents. The illness got its name because it spreads rapidly in areas where dogs are housed in close proximity to each other, such as boarding kennels or dog shows. Prevention by vaccination is best. If your dog is often in kennels or exposed to other dogs, repeat twice a year.

CAUSES

• Dogs can pick up the disease anywhere there are other dogs, but they can also get it from exposure to a single infected dog.

• Most cases are triggered by the bacterium known as *Bordetella bronchoseptica*, which invades and infects the body after the virus has taken hold.

• Other viruses, including canine parainfluenza, can be involved, as may other bacteria.

WHAT YOU AND YOUR VET CAN DO

Treatment is symptomatic, geared to relieve coughing and prevent secondary bacterial infections. Most cases will spontaneously resolve themselves within two to three weeks, but owners can make their dogs more comfortable with a cough suppressant obtained from the vet.

SYMPTOMS

• The major sign is a dry, hacking cough. You may suspect the dog has caught something in its throat or that it is trying to vomit. The cough may be accompanied by retching and gagging.
• Touching the throat will set off the cough. Use a harness instead of a collar and leash to avoid putting pressure on the throat.

COMPLEMENTARY TREATMENTS

⊠ HERBAL REMEDIES
Regular doses of a herbal cough suppressant like slippery elm may help. Gently run the syrup into the mouth using a 5 ml syringe without a needle.

▢ HOMEOPATHIC REMEDIES
Ipecacuanha 6c should give relief when there is constant coughing. Alternatively *Drosera* 6c (sundew) may be helpful. Dose the dog twice daily for up to five days, and then twice weekly until the symptoms have disappeared.

THE DIGESTIVE SYSTEM

Disturbances of the stomach and intestines in dogs have a variety of causes, including ingestion of bad food and or foreign objects; bacterial and viral infections; parasites, especially worms; allergies; and diseases of other organs (kidney, liver, pancreas and diabetes). Common signs may include vomiting, diarrhoea, constipation, appetite loss and abdominal pain. Most cases diagnosed and treated early on respond well to diet changes and medication. Chronic (long-term) cases require more time and patience. Never force-feed your dog, but give specific meals at least twice a day, taking careful note of what your dog actually eats. A change in appetite or bowel consistency is often one of the earliest signs of a problem.

A BALANCED DIET

Proper nutrition is vital to good health in your dog. Commercially available premium foods are convenient. and their composition is strictly controlled and regulated by commercial suppliers. The label should clearly state that the food is nutritionally complete and balanced for the lifestyle and age of the dog. Choose between foods that are labelled "growth" for puppies, "maintenance" for adults, and "senior" for golden years. Feeding-trial results to back up the claims should also be available if you ask for them.

2

In general, all dogs should eat at least two meals a day. Meals should be of a specific amount, left out for 20–30 minutes and then removed. Let your dog's body weight and physical condition be your guide on what and how much to feed.

Keep snacks to less than 5 percent of its total diet and feed only healthy snacks like grated or chopped carrots and other fresh vegetables. Home-made natural diets take more time but are well worth the effort. The key is to find a recipe that keeps your dog healthy and appeals to its taste buds.

YOUR DOG'S DAILY REQUIREMENTS

• Daily caloric requirements vary with age, activity, and metabolic rate. Average needs for an adult house dog are: small (7–16 kg) 600–900 calories: medium (16–25 kg) 900–1500 calories; large (25–38 kg) 1500–2000 calories.
• Carbohydrates are the dog's main source of energy. They need to be cooked to make them easier to digest.
• Fat is a further source of energy. Some fatty acids, such as linoleic acid, are essential to the dog's diet, as they cannot be manufactured in the body.

• Proteins are used for building and repairing muscle. Some components of protein—the amino acids—must be present to avoid a deficiency.
• At least 13 vitamins are necessary to a dog's health. Dogs are generally able to manufacture their own vitamin C.
• Minerals are vital not just for promoting healthy bones, but also for the smooth working of a variety of metabolic processes in the body, such as the correct functioning of the thyroid glands.

TYPES OF FOOD

• Canned foods have the best taste, but also cost the most. They contain the most water (60–80 percent) and the least preservatives. Canned foods are cooked to 49°C, which sterilizes them so they stay fresh for over one year.

• Dried foods are convenient and economical, but only stay fresh for six months. They have the most preservatives, which act as antioxidants to prevent fat from becoming rancid. It is vital that your dog has access to clean drinking water at all times, and this is especially important when it is eating dry food. Without sufficient fluid your pet is likely to end up seriously dehydrated, and may possibly suffer kidney problems as a consequence.

• Semi-moist foods contain about 35 percent water. They stay fresh for nine months and contain propylene glycol as the source of carbohydrate, water and preservative. They also have antioxidants added to prevent the fat from turning rancid. As the preservative is sugar-based, these foods are not recommended for a diabetic dog.

• Nothing can replace a wholesome well-balanced diet but proper supplementation can make a great diet even healthier. In addition, common problems such as arthritis and "ageing changes"—such as poor coat and decreased activity—do not always improve when diet alone is changed. By identifying specific problems and providing additional nutritional support through supplements, many such conditions can be helped. Do not be tempted to give too many, however, because it could actually be harmful to your pet's health.

2

Dried foods are the least palatable for a dog.

Meat-based foods can tempt fussy eaters.

VOMITING

2

Vomiting that occurs occasionally in a healthy dog is generally not a cause for concern. The most common cause of vomiting in dogs is the habit of eating indiscriminately. However, persistent vomiting with or without signs of illness such as appetite loss, depression or lethargy, diarrhoea, or constipation means it's time to call your vet so that you can identify the problem. Severe dehydration resulting from vomiting can lead to more serious problems if left untreated. Vomiting brings up a mixture of food, acids, and enzymes from the stomach or intestines. During vomiting, you will see the dog's abdominal muscles contracting, which differentiates vomiting from regurgitation.

CAUSES

- Dietary indiscretion: rubbish, excess fatty foods, and table scraps.
- Foreign objects: bones, rubber balls, stones.
- Parasites: round worms (see p. 38), especially in puppies.
- Viral infections: distemper (see p. 22) and parvovirus (see p. 31).
- Diseases: diabetes (see p. 69), cancer and ulcers are often associated with blood in vomit.
- Toxins: household drugs, rat poison, antifreeze, pesticides.
- Motion sickness (in a car).
- Stress/emotions: excess excitement or upset.

SYMPTOMS

Prior to vomiting:
- Excess salivation,
- Discomfort,
- Pacing and whining,
- Gurgling or loud stomach noises.

WHAT YOU AND YOUR VET CAN DO

- There is a difference between vomiting and regurgitation, which is the spontaneous reflux of food before it reaches the stomach. It indicates a problem in the oesophagus (a constriction or obstruction) and must be treated by a vet. The food comes up immediately after it is eaten and looks exactly as it did when it was eaten. It is common in puppies as they begin eating solid food and occurs effortlessly, surprising the dog as much as it does you.

- After a bout of vomiting, withhold food and water for 12–24 hours. Giving either at this time makes vomiting worse. Allow your dog to lick ice cubes occasionally, or give it small amounts of chicken broth. You can give a liquid bland diet of white puréed chicken or turkey breast in small amounts from day two, four to six times daily. Add cooked brown rice and raw chopped greens. After the third day, gradually add in some of your dog's normal diet, about a quarter at a time, feeding three to four times a day. By the end of the week the number of meals should be back to twice daily.

• For mild vomiting, mix eight tablespoons of fresh minced parsley with one cup of water. Boil for five minutes, strain and cool. Add one teaspoon of honey per cup. Give one tablespoon to the dog every 10 minutes. Alternatively, pour two cups of boiling water over eight tablespoons of fresh thyme or rosemary and leave to infuse for 10 minutes. Strain and cool, and give one teaspoon every 10 minutes. Then dose with one teaspoon of Rescue Remedy every hour for about four hours. Let the dog fast on honey water (one tablespoon of honey in one litre of warm water) for the rest of the day. Feed light meat or vegetable broth the next day, reintroducing solid foods slowly thereafter.

• If vomiting persists in your dog, see your vet who will carry out a physical examination and discuss with you the history of the vomiting. Blood tests can rule out diseases of the liver and kidney, diabetes, cancer or allergies. An X ray of the abdomen can outline a foreign object and also rule out cancer.

2

Warning

If your dog persists in eating grass, and then vomiting, this can be a sign that it is has intestinal worms. Should you notice any blood in the vomit, consult your vet without delay. A puppy that keeps being sick should be seen within a day because of the risk of a foreign body or dehydration. Never try and treat your dog with household drugs, such as aspirin.

COMPLEMENTARY TREATMENTS

🗀 HOMEOPATHIC REMEDIES

For moderate vomiting *Nux vomica* 6c (poison nut) can help: one pellet every four hours until symptoms are gone. If there is no effect in 24 hours, try *Pulsatilla* 6c (windflower): one pellet every four hours until symptoms are gone. In each case, give no food 10 minutes before or after the treatment.

DIARRHOEA

Diarrhoea consists of abnormal, frequent passage of loose or soft stools, and is one of the most common signs of disease in dogs. It occurs when dissolved substances within the intestine cause excess water to move into the intestine. This accumulation decreases the absorption of food, called malabsorption. It may also cause increased secretion of electrolytes into the intestine, called maldigestion. Diarrhoea lasting less than 24 hours without signs of illness can be beneficial. It is the body's defence mechanism to cleanse itself. If it lasts more than 24 hours, with or without signs of illness, you should take your dog to your vet.

Scavenging for food in rubbish bins can lead to vomiting and diarrhoea.

CAUSES

- Dietary indiscretion (including foreign objects).
- Stress.
- Chronic disease.
- Parasites (especially in puppies).
- Allergy.

SYMPTOMS

- Passage of loose stools.
- Increased frequency of passage.
- General depression.
- Increased thirst.
- Blood-stained faeces.

WHAT YOU CAN DO

- Feed small, bland, low-fat, easily digestible meals four times daily. Use lean protein (poultry or fish). On the first day leave the dog to fast for 12–24 hours, but give fluids to prevent dehydration and to replace electrolytes (sodium, potassium). On day two feed your dog chicken purée. Add live yogurt or acidophilus cultures to replace beneficial intestinal bacteria lost with diarrhoea. On day three add vegetables to the broth to increase fibre. Fibre acts like a sponge and draws water out of stool to firm it up. On day four add white rice (grain) and on day five change from white rice to brown rice. On day six begin adding normal diet into this, a quarter at a time over three days.

Live yogurt can settle the gut.

WHAT YOUR VET CAN DO

• The vet can make a thorough physical examination of your dog, checking the dog's history with you. It's helpful if you can note when the diarrhoea began, how often it occurs, if the dog is straining, the character of the stool (bloody, black, with mucus), and if the dog ate anything unusual. The vet can also make a faecal check for worms—these are especially common in puppies.

• Diagnostics for long-term and/or recurrent cases of diarrhoea with or without weight loss may include blood tests (to rule out systemic disease, bacterial or viral); X rays to find an offensive object or cancerous growth; examination of stool cultures to reveal bacteria (such as salmonella); and intestinal biopsies.

PARVOVIRUS

• Parvovirus is a fatal infectious disease of dogs worldwide. although it is now manageable through vaccination. The virus is most contagious and is spread by contact with infected faeces. Parvovirus attacks the lining of the intestinal tract and the heart of young puppies. Signs of parvovirus include vomiting, vile-smelling diarrhoea generally with blood, and collapse.

• Prompt veterinary treatment is essential; most puppies without immunization die. Intravenous fluids are essential to replace losses in vomit and diarrhoea. All other medication should be given intravenously until vomiting stops. Once vomiting stops, you can start giving fluids by mouth and a bland diet.

COMPLEMENTARY TREATMENTS

⊠ HERBAL REMEDIES
To control diarrhoea, add two acidophilus capsules to each meal until the stool is firm. Alternatively, treat with pills made from eight tablespoons of chopped sage leaves and two finely crushed cloves of garlic. Mix with honey and roll into small balls. Give these three times a day: one pill for small dogs or two to four pills for large dogs. A small quantity of activated charcoal, sold in pharmacies, will absorb toxins and poisons. Dissolve up to three tablets in water (depending on the size of your dog) and give them to your dog to drink. Use for a day or two only, because charcoal can affect absorption of beneficial substances into the body.

⊡ HOMEOPATHIC REMEDIES
For small, freqent bowel movements try *Arsenicum album* 6c (arsenic trioxide): one pellet every four hours for three treatments. Allow no food 10 minutes before or after treatment.

Activated charcoal tablets

CONSTIPATION

2

Constipation occurs occasionally in dogs. Constipation is infrequent or absent defecation occurring with retention of faeces in the rectum and colon. Older and less active dogs are prone to this. Signs that your dog may have constipation include straining to defecate, with or without dry faeces. The causes of constipation include indiscriminate eating (e.g. rubbish, disposable nappies); lack of fibre (roughage or bulk) in the diet; lack of water (dehydration); lack of exercise; illness and obesity. It is also possible that the dog may be suffering from kidney disease, tumours, an anal sac abscess, or pelvic fracture.

WHAT YOU CAN DO

• Increase the fibre in your dog's diet. Add fresh vegetables (four tablespoons of grated raw vegetables per 4.5 kg), cooked brown rice or wheat bran to the usual dog food. Raw meat acts as a natural laxative. For long-term prevention buy or make food with greater than 10 percent fibre (as indicated on the label). Also increase your dog's fluid intake—offer it water, chicken broth, or fruit juices.

• Make sure your dog gets plenty of exercise, which increases blood flow to the organs.

• Consult your vet to determine the underlying cause of the constipation and its treatment.

Constipation tends to affect older dogs that don't drink enough plain water.

COMPLEMENTARY TREATMENTS

⊠ HERBAL REMEDIES

Add 30 ml (2 tbsp) of sunflower oil to the evening meal (three to four x 15 ml for large dogs). In stubborn cases, in small dogs, soak four pitted prunes in water and give with oats porridge and a little milk. Large dogs should have six to eight pitted prunes prepared in the same way.
Plant oats and wheat in mixed borders for dogs to eat. Make sure that there is grass growing for them to eat too.

☐ HOMEOPATHIC REMEDIES

To counteract a bad diet, give Nux vomica 6c (poison nut): one pellet every 12 hours over three days. For poorly nourished dogs, try Silicea 6c (silicon dioxide/tissue salt): one pellet every 12 hours over three days. Allow no food 10 minutes before or after the treatments.

BLOAT

Bloat is a true life-and-death emergency in dogs. The stomach fills with air and fluid (simple bloat) and may or may not rotate (complex bloat). Large, deep-chested breeds are predisposed to bloat, although the exact causes are unknown. A typical scenario is that the dog eats a big meal, drinks a lot of water, then goes outside to play. When it comes back inside it has a large, distended abdomen and is salivating, retching and belching. Gradually it becomes restless (getting up and lying down repeatedly), depressed, weak, and finally collapses. The diagnosis of bloat is made by taking the history of the dog, noting signs, and taking an X ray.

2

WHAT YOU AND YOUR VET CAN DO

• To treat simple bloat a tube is passed into the stomach to decompress the air. The dog is fine instantly.

• With complex bloat a stomach tube cannot pass into the stomach because the oesophagus is twisted. Surgery is necessary here, to attach the stomach to the body wall so that if the dog bloats again the stomach will not rotate.

• Prevention is the key because recurrence is common. Feed small amounts of food three to four times a day instead of one large meal. After eating, limit water intake, since the rapid mixing of food and water in the stomach causes excess gas to form. Do not allow exercise one hour before or two hours after eating.

SYMPTOMS

• Increased salivation.
• Sudden onset of severe pain and distress.
• Distended abdomen.

COMPLEMENTARY TREATMENTS

⊠ HERBAL REMEDIES
Although bloat is an emergency condition that needs rapid veterinary attention, giving fresh cabbage juice can bring relief at the outset.

☐ HOMEOPATHIC REMEDIES
Nux moschata 30c (nutmeg) taken every quarter of an hour for 45 minutes may be beneficial. *Carbo vegetabilis* 30c (charcoal) can be especially valuable for counteracting not just the build-up of gas, but also the accompanying shock.

FOOD ALLERGIES

Food allergy is an abnormal reaction to a dietary ingredient, often a protein source. Signs that your dog may have a food allergy include bladder infections (e.g. cystitis); digestive problems such as vomiting and diarrhoea; and itching, which is often associated with secondary bacterial skin infections and can result in red oozing areas and scabs.

CAUSES

One-third of common food allergies may be due to a protein component of a food. Common food allergens include beef, dairy products (milk, cheese, and eggs), chicken, wheat, corn, and tofu (which can be a cause of soy allergy). Even snacks and flavoured vitamins can be the cause of adverse reactions, so you need to be aware of everything your dog eats. As any dog owner knows, they lack discrimination.

WHAT YOU CAN DO

• The only way to find out the true cause of a food allergy is to use an elimination diet. A single source of protein is used for 12 weeks to see if the dog's condition improves. After this new ingredients are added back into the diet one at a time every five to seven days until the problem recurs. You have to keep a note of what was given when so you will know which one caused the problem to return.

• For the elimination diet to work, you must use a protein to which your dog has never before been exposed, such as lamb, rabbit, mutton or venison.

• Always use distilled water or boil tap water and then refrigerate it. Avoid chlorine because it can cause an allergic reaction.

• You can also try a raw meat diet because raw meat does not cause the same allergic reaction that cooked meat does.

• Food allergies tend to be lifelong, but once you identify the offending allergen you will be able find many suitable diets that do not include the problem foods but still provide a balanced diet. Ask your vet for suggestions.

COMPLEMENTARY TREATMENTS

⊡ HOMEOPATHIC REMEDIES
Vitamin C in high does acts as an antihistimine and may help with itching, if present. A daily dosage of 1000 mg is recommended.

Adding vitamin B complex to the daily diet is also useful. Give the dog a quarter to one tablet each day, depending on the dog's size.

SCOOTING

If you see your dog scooting or dragging its backside across the floor, licking or biting at its anal area, anal sacs may be the problem. These are located on either side of the anus and contain a semi-liquid, vile-smelling material that is normally squeezed out and emptied along with the faeces. Sometimes the anal sacs do not empty properly. The ducts can become clogged and infection, impaction or an abscess can develop, causing severe pain.

2

SYMPTOMS

- Your dog drags itself along with its front paws while in a sitting position.
- Biting and nibbling at the anal area.
- Glandular deposits may start to solidify and become infected, with abscesses developing and bursting out near the surface of the anus.

WHAT YOU AND YOUR VET CAN DO

• In most cases, manual expression of the anal sacs solves the problem. Medication can be used to relieve inflammation and treat any infection. Occasionally, with recurrent and persistent problems, sacculectomy (surgical removal of the anal sacs) may be the kindest and most cost-effective solution. Ask your vet to check the anal sacs as often as once a month in recurrent cases to prevent impaction and abscesses forming.

• Apply hot packs to relieve the pain. Alternatively, soak the dog twice a day for 10 minutes in a tub of fairly hot water containing one or two cups of Epsom salts. Rinse off and apply a thin layer of petroleum jelly or mineral oil to the anal area.

COMPLEMENTARY TREATMENTS

⊠ HERBAL REMEDIES
Increasing dietary fibre promotes natural anal sac expression. Add fibre with grains (such as oats) and seeds and also make sure your dog has regular exercise since a lean body may help to reduce anal sac problems.

Oat bran

▢ HOMEOPATHIC REMEDIES
Silicea 6c (twice a day for three days) can be useful for scooting. If there are signs of an abscess, then *Hepar sulphuris calcareum* 30c is recommended.
Initially, these treatments are usually given daily for five days; ensure the sacs are emptied by your vet as well, to reduce the risk of a recurrence.

2

OBESITY

Experts say that almost half of all dogs are clinically obese—which means they are 15 percent above their ideal weight. This potentially reduces its life span and predisposes it to several life-threatening diseases. In general, more female dogs are affected than males. There are hormonal and genetic influences as well as individual variations in metabolism and appetite, but the reason why dogs are obese are the owners who indulge their pets with treats and give them oversized portions at mealtimes.

CAUSES

- Overeating.
- Inactivity.
- Neutering—can lead to weight gain.
- Hormonal problem.

YOUR DOG'S WEIGHT

- To tell if your dog is overweight, give it a rib check—you should be able to feel but not see each rib. It should also have a waist, which should be tucked up behind its rib cage. If your dog has lost its waist or if you can pinch more than an inch, it's time to cut back.

- It's easier to prevent your dog gaining excess weight than it is to lose it. Regular visits to your vet should include monitoring your pet's weight.

- Before beginning your dog on any weight-loss programme, talk it through with your vet. it is important to rule out medical problems that mimic obesity, such as heart and liver disease, hypothyroidism, and Cushing's disease.

Warning

If your dog is not used to a lot of exercise, it is not a good idea to take it on long hikes. Instead, gradually build up its level of fitness through regular walks. This will be much better than exhausting it with the occasional marathon.

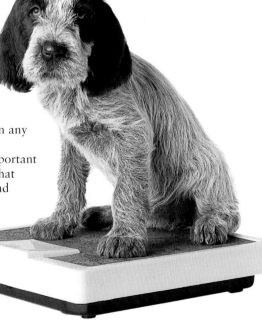

Regular weighing is the best way of finding out if your dog the right size for its age.

WHAT YOU CAN DO

• You should feed your dog a high-protein, high-fibre (over 15 percent), low-fat (less than 10 percent) diet. Increasing the fibre provides bulk which fills it up and keeps it happy while losing weight. You will need to decrease your dog's total number of calories by 20 percent at the same time. To control fatty acid build-up, give one to two kelp tablets daily. Set a maximum initial weight loss at 15 percent and calculate your feedings and exercise to achieve this.

• Increase the number of meals up to six per day—the more meals the dog eats, the more its metabolism is stimulated to burn calories. When you feed your dog, leave the food out for 20 minutes and then remove it. Don't give table scraps and keep snacks to less than 5 percent of the diet. Try healthy snacks of fresh vegetables such as white asparagus tips.

• Monitor your dog's weight weekly: keep a chart on your refrigerator door along with a "before' photo. When your pet reaches its ideal target weight, change it over to a "light" diet. Continue to monitor its weight carefully for the next 60 days. Record its weight once a month for the first six months, then four times a year.

• Aim for a minimum of 20 minutes a day exercise. Two 10-minute walks is a start and you can gradually build up from there. It may be useful to find a dog fitness centre that offers a complete package for flabby pets.

INTESTINAL WORMS

The most common intestinal parasites affecting dogs are roundworms, hookworms, whipworms and tapeworms. Roundworms and hookworms can be transmitted to humans, where they can migrate or move to the intestine, eye, brain, or other organs, possibly causing blindness, organ damage, and in rare cases death.

2

SYMPTOMS

- Young puppies born with a heavy burden of roundworms often suffer a cough, rough haircoat and pot belly. Occasionally they vomit and have diarrhoea.
- As they grow older, their growth is likely to be stunted, and they may suffer from vomiting, diarrhoea and a swollen abdomen.
- In the case of tapeworms, the white segments containing eggs may be seen around the anal area. Tapeworms cause few symptoms, although the dog may nibble at the anus if there is heavy infestation.
- Signs of the presence of whipworms are diarrhoea and loss of weight.

CAUSES

Roundworm

- All puppies are born with roundworms in their lungs. Puppies can pass the eggs in their faeces from three weeks onward. If these eggs are then swallowed after being excreted, further infection results. Ingestion of eggs on the ground can also result in hookworm and whipworm infestations. Normally the eggs and worms are microscopic but in severe infestations the worms may appear in the vomit or diarrhoea of infected puppies.

- Fleas transmit tapeworms. The flea deposits the larval form of the tapeworm in the dog's blood, prior to withdrawing its blood meal. Three months later you will find flat white tapeworm segments in the dog's stool.

Tapeworm

- Whipworms are 5 cm (2 inches) long, no thicker than a thread, and look like whips. They are the leading cause of chronic diarrhoea and weight loss in dogs. Dogs become infected by ingesting the microscopic eggs in the soil. The worms attach to the wall of the large intestine and mature over the next 10 weeks.

WHAT YOUR VET CAN DO

- Worms are easily diagnosed by a microscopic examination of your dog's stool.

- Safe, effective treatments for all worm problems are available through your vet. Regular worming, with annual faecal check-ups, is the best way to keep your dog healthy and worm-free. Female dogs with litters of puppies should routinely be wormed at two, four, six, and eight weeks of age.

Warning

The roundworm *Toxocara canis* also represents a serious threat to the health of children in particular, which is why deworming of puppies is so vital. If swallowed, there is a possibility that the resulting larvae that hatch in the intestinal tract will then migrate around the body, and could cause blindness. Children must always be taught to wash their hands thoroughly before touching food, with toddlers being at greatest risk.

WHAT YOU CAN DO

• Routine examinations of your dog's stools are the best way to prevent worm infestations.

• Picking up your dog's faeces helps prevent environmental contamination. It is illegal in many public areas to allow your dog to soil without cleaning up its mess because of the associated public health risks. Be sure that your children do not play in areas where dogs habitually defecate.

• Keep the dog's surroundings scrupulously clean of all flies, fleas, poultry and bird droppings.

2

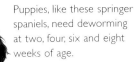

Puppies, like these springer spaniels, need deworming at two, four, six and eight weeks of age.

COMPLEMENTARY TREATMENTS

✄ HERBAL REMEDIES

Crush one clove of garlic and mix with seven minced pumpkin seeds, one sprig of thyme and some honey. Roll into balls and give all at once to the dog.

Alternatively, sprinkle between a quarter and one teaspoonful of ground pumpkin seeds over food.

☐ HOMEOPATHIC REMEDIES

Cina 3x (wormseed) taken three times daily for a minimum period of three weeks can help clear roundworms. Faecal screening can then be used to see if the dog is free from the obvious signs of these parasites. This remedy may also have some effect against tapeworms but *Filix mas* 3x (male fern) is the usual treatment for these, used on a similar basis to *Cina*.

Pumpkin seeds

PANCREATIC PROBLEMS

The pancreas is a vital organ located close to the small intestine and connected to it. Through this connection, it discharges digestive enzymes that assist in the breakdown of food into the gut. This function is quite separate from its production of the hormones insulin and glucagon in the endocrine system (see p. 68).

Pancreatitis is severe inflammation of the pancreas that often occurs in dogs that eat too much rich, fatty food or get bad food from rubbish. Miniature Schnauzers and obese dogs have the highest incidence of this disease. Dogs allowed to sample the feast at holiday celebrations often end up with indigestion and pancreatitis. With repeated episodes of inflammation, the pancreas is not able to function properly, which may lead to diabetes mellitus (see p. 68) and other problems such as pancreatic insufficiency (see p. 89)

WHAT YOU AND YOUR VET CAN DO

• Diagnosis is based on history, signs, and blood tests if necessary. If diabetes is a problem both blood glucose (sugar) and urine sugar are elevated. Treatment is geared to allow the intestinal tract to rest by withholding all food and water for up to 24 hours. Fluids may be given subcutaneously, or—if the dog is severely dehydrated—intravenously. Most dogs respond to treatment and in a few days are gradually put back on to food, starting with a bland diet in small portions.

SYMPTOMS

• Vomiting.
• Diarrhoea.
• Abdominal pain.
• Depression and lethargy.

• Prevention using moderation is the best policy. Avoid fatty foods and feed several small meals daily. If necessary use a digestive enzyme supplement containing lipase, protease, and amylase.

COMPLEMENTARY TREATMENTS

✖ HERBAL REMEDIES
The use of yarrow (*Achillea millefolium*) can bring some relief, particularly where there is also bad diarrhoea. Fresh yarrow leaves can be chopped and added to your dog's food, three times daily for up to one week.

☐ HOMEOPATHIC REMEDIES
Iris versicolor 6x may help to overcome the effects of pancreatitis. Your vet will usually recommend that you treat your dog every four hours until the symptoms have disappeared. If this preparation is working, there should be some relief within a day.

SKIN AND HAIR

Skin diseases are very common in dogs. They can occur because of bacterial, fungal, allergic, parasitic and hormonal disorders. In older dogs cancer, skin tumours and cysts are also common. Signs of skin problems are among the easiest to detect—they include dry flaky skin, as well as red and irritated areas of hair loss with scabs and crusts. However, skin diseases can have similar signs which makes diagnosis difficult. Also, unfortunately, many skin diseases are chronic and cannot be cured, but they can be controlled. These cases often require long-term treatment in which nutrition, bathing and grooming will provide relief for your pet.

GOOD GROOMING

Regular grooming helps keep your dog's skin and haircoat healthy. It helps eliminate mats and tangles and gives you a chance to check for fleas and ticks, as well as lumps and bumps. Shedding hair is a natural process. Indoor lighting and heating, as well as seasonal temperature variations all affect it. Most healthy dogs shed twice a year in the spring and autumn, while some breeds, like the Pekingese and rough collie, shed all year round. Skin disorders, dietary imbalances, and hormonal fluctuations all affect hair growth and shedding cycles.

HAIR TYPES AND CARE

• How often your dog needs to be bathed and groomed will vary depending on the breed, the hair length and the dog's lifestyle. Breeds like the Pekingese and rough collie, need weekly brushing and regular grooming to help remove dead hair all year round.

• Breeds with fancy haircuts, like poodles and cocker spaniels, need attention every four to six weeks. Poodles shed but their hair does not come out until it is brushed. Breeds like the Maltese and Yorkshire Terrier, with long flowing skirts, need attention every couple of weeks to prevent hair becoming matted.

• For short-coated breeds like retrievers and shepherds, grooming every three to four months is fine.

• Regardless of the breed, the bath is the single most important step in grooming. Some indoor dogs have to be bathed more often to keep them clean.

In general, the more hair a dog has, the more coat care it will require all year long.

3

You may find grooming easier when the dog's on a lead. Leave 45 cm (18 inches) of slack in the chain so your pet has some movement.

3

WHAT YOU CAN DO

• It is important to use products that are specifically designed for dogs. Your vet may recommend the best products for your dog's skin and haircoat. Proper grooming equipment also makes the job easier. A slicker brush, along with a metal comb, a pin brush, and bristle brush work well for most breeds initially.

• Before the bath, brush out the coat. This helps remove mats, which are twice as hard to get out once wet. Lubricate your dog's eyes with artificial tears, or one drop of vitamin E oil, and put a cotton ball in each ear. Rinse the dog down and shampoo it twice. If using a medicated shampoo, leave the second set of suds on for five to ten minutes so that you get the most out of it. Apply a conditioner, and give the dog a final rinse.

• Your dog may or may not tolerate being dried, by towel or hairdryer. In either case, you should keep it inside until it is dry and then brush out its coat. Brushing the fur backward helps to remove excess undercoat. This is a good time to wipe out your dog's ears—use cotton balls and an appropriate ear cleaning solution.

A set of grooming brushes is essential for keeping your dog's coat in good condition.

FLEAS

Fleas are the most common cause of itching and skin irritation in dogs. Over 50 percent of all skin allergies in dogs are due to a severe reaction to fleas' saliva. If these dogs are bitten by a flea they will lose hair and itch until they are raw. Most also end up with secondary bacterial skin infections which need treatment. In addition, fleas suck blood and can cause anaemia. They also transmit tapeworms.

Fleas cause irritation, but can be killed off.

WHAT YOU CAN DO

• Signs of fleas include itching, especially at the base of the tail, and tiny black specks that look like dirt. To confirm this "dirt" is caused by fleas, place it on a moist cotton ball. Flea dirt will turn red because of the blood it contains.

• Once your dog has been diagnosed with a flea problem, you need to treat all the pets in your house as well as the rooms. Vacuum the carpets and throw away the filled bag immediately so that flea eggs do not hatch in it. For your carpeting, insect-growth regulators like fenoxycarb or methoprene last up to one and a half years. Or you can sprinkle borax onto the carpet, then vacuum. Be sure to wash your dog's bedding with hot soapy water. Finally, bathe all the animals living in your home. Use a flea shampoo with pyrethrins or d-limolene as the active ingredient.

• Outside your house, natural products that contain nematodes are best. Nematodes are live microscopic worms that eat the larval and pupal forms of fleas and 250 other pests. Spray your patio, especially the dark, damp areas that are fleas' favourite places.

Scratching indicates the presence of fleas.

SYMPTOMS

• Itching.
• Flea dirt.
• Hair loss at the top of the tail.

Warning

Often cat fleas will infest a dog. Take care with chemical treatments such as powders, however, because not all are suitable for both dogs and cats. Medicated shampoos are easier to use on dogs, while powders are better for cats.

3

WHAT YOUR VET CAN DO

• Today flea prevention is the key to flea control. Your vet can prescribe one of the new monthly products available. Program is a product that contains luferuron, which causes fleas to lay sterile eggs and prevents environmental contamination. Program is very safe and has been approved in 35 countries. Prevention should start in the spring, when the outdoor temperature hits 18–20°C regularly. This is the best way to prevent a flea problem starting.

• Fleas live primarily in its surroundings and not on the dog. They stay on the dog only long enough to get a blood meal and then jump to the ground to lay more eggs. If you see one flea on your dog, a thousand more are around the corner (somewhere in your house): this is why prevention is so important.

3

Fleas are most commonly found in a triangular area that runs down the back to the top of the tail.

COMPLEMENTARY TREATMENTS

⊠HERBAL REMEDIES

To make a lemon flea dip, peel an entire lemon into thin slices, boil in 600 ml (1 pint) of water, and steep overnight. Cool and use as a dip or daily spritz. A natural herbal itch remedy can be made with cats' claw, licorice root, and dandelion: mix five drops of each then give three drops of the final solution once daily for 14 days. You can give the dog this by mouth or mix it in its food. *Diatomaceous earth*, which is derived from microscopic algae, can help to kill fleas safely in the home by dehydrating them on contact. Apply this product to the floor (it's advisable to wear a mask), paying particular attention to places such as the gap between carpeting and walls where fleas often lurk.

⊡HOMEOPATHIC REMEDIES

Sulphur 30c may help the dog to resist further infection: one dose of two whole pellets or three pellets crushed to powder every 30 days. If this is not effective, try the same dose of *Psorinum* 30c. Give no food to your dog 60 minutes before or after treatments.

MANGE

There are two types of mange that can afflict dogs. Demodectic mange is caused by microscopic mites that normally live in the skin. It causes very little itching, although secondary bacterial skin infections are common, which do cause irritation. Sarcoptic mange, or scabies, is also caused by mites, but these mites dig tiny tunnels under the skin and this causes intense itching. Dogs with scabies itch, dig and bite at themselves ferociously.

Demodex mites

DEMODECTIC MANGE

• There are two forms of demodectic mange in dogs: localized and generalized. The localized form causes hair loss on the face and front legs. This form is common in puppies. It does not itch and often resolves spontaneously in four to eight weeks. Occasionally it gets worse and progresses into the generalized form.

• The generalized form of demodectic mange can affect the whole body and is more common in older dogs. Secondary bacterial skin infections and itching are common. The ears and feet may also be severely infected.

• Young dogs of three to six months old may have an inherited predisposition to demodectic mange. High risk breeds include the shar pei, west highland white terrier, great Dane and airedale. Older dogs can get demodectic mange if their immune system is depressed because of drugs or an underlying disease such as cancer.

SARCOPTIC MANGE

• The skin of dogs with scabies gets oozing sores, with hair loss, crusts and scabs. Secondary bacterial infections are common. Initially the itching and hair loss are most pronounced on the ear tips, elbows, legs and face. In dogs these mites like to burrow deep into the skin. That makes them extremely hard to find, even with deep skin scrapings and biopsies.

• These cases are often misdiagnosed as allergies with secondary bacterial skin infections.

Urban foxes carry sarcoptic mange, which can be spread to humans as well as dogs.

LICE

Lice are tiny, six-legged parasites that feed on blood and can cause anemia. Weak, run-down puppies are most susceptible. If you look carefully at the dog's hair you may see tiny white spots which are the egg casings. Lice spend their entire life on the animal and are not transferrable to other pets or people. They do not infest your home and primarily occur in the cooler winter months.

SYMPTOMS

- Itching.
- White nits in hair.
- Anaemia (pale gum colour in a weak, drowsy puppy).

3

WHAT YOU AND YOUR VET CAN DO

- Once the presence of lice has been confirmed, treatment is relatively straightforward and is similar to that for fleas (see p. 44). Most products that kill fleas also kill lice.

- Bathe the puppy with d-limolene or pyrethrin shampoo. This kills adult lice but not eggs, so repeat the baths weekly until all the eggs are gone. Leave the suds on the dog for five to ten minutes. Pyrethrin dips are also effective for lice and fleas.

- Improve the general health of your puppy by adding brewer's yeast to its diet (5–15 ml/1 tsp–1 tbsp, depending on the puppy's size).

- Itching can be controlled with antihistamines—ask your vet's advice. Vitamin C in high doses also acts as an antihistamine.

- If anaemia is diagnosed, treatment will be with B vitamins and iron.

COMPLEMENTARY TREATMENTS

⊠ HERBAL REMEDIES
Chrysanthemums contain pyrethrins which are effective against fleas and lice. Citrus fruits such as lemons contain d-limolene which is also effective.

▢ HOMEOPATHIC REMEDIES
Sulphur 30c can help to lower the risk of reinfection.

TICKS

Ticks are small insects that prey on the blood of people, dogs, cats, deer, horses and rodents. They are carriers for a wide range of blood parasites and other harmful microbes, which they transmit while feeding. Dogs that live, or are exercised, in rural areas, especially on heathland where both domestic farm stock and grazing animals such as deer are to be found, are most vulnerable. Such herbivores are the normal host of ticks, but on occasion these parasites will transfer to other hosts, such as your dog.

Ticks swell after feeding.

The ticks attach themselves to the dog's leg and may then move up the body. Once ticks puncture the dog's skin and start to swell with blood, they rapidly increase in size.

Lyme disease is transferred to animals and people through the bite of the deer tick. It can cause intermittent lameness, fever, heart and kidney disease, as well as disorders of the nervous system.

3

Working dogs are most at risk from ticks, since farm animals, such as sheep, are the normal hosts of these parasites.

WHAT YOU CAN DO

• If there are only a few ticks on your pet, they can be removed by applying alcohol or tick spray directly to the ticks to kill them. Wait a few minutes and then grasp the tick as close to the skin as possible with tweezers and carefully remove it from the dog by applying steady traction until it releases its hold. Because ticks can carry diseases that are infectious to humans, wear gloves and wash your hands well after treatment.

• Another method of removing ticks is to wipe the parasite's body with petroleum jelly, paying special attention to its rear end, where its breathing pore is located. Once this is effectively blocked by the jelly, the tick will no longer be able to breathe properly and will loosen its grip, ultimately dropping off without complications.

• Occasionally the tick mouthparts remain attached to the skin of the dog and cannot be removed by tweezers or by using jelly. This may cause a local reaction that clears up on its own after a few days and is usually not a cause for concern. It is rare for a tick bite to become infected.

Petroleum jelly is ideal for removing ticks.

• If your dog has a heavy tick infestation, then a commercial insecticide preparation such as a tick dip should be used. Several dips will probably be required. Topical products used every month will eliminate ticks on the dog. To keep your animals safe, talk to your vet to find out the safest and most effective products.

3

LICK GRANULOMA

A lick granuloma is a skin lesion usually located on the wrist area of a front leg. Occasionally it is found on the front or outside of the rear leg just above the paw area. In all cases, it is an area the dog can reach by licking, which it does so continuously and compulsively.

CAUSES

• The true underlying cause of lick granuloma remains unknown, although a combination of medical and psychological factors appears to be responsible. The lesions are thought to be due to stress or boredom in some dogs and even to be an obsessive/compulsive disorder in others. The dog's licking helps pass the time.

• Psychological stimuli such as separation anxiety (see p. 84), a new pet or child in the home, or neighbour dogs invading the dog's "territory" can create psychological stress. Self-stimulation such as picking out an area to concentrate on and licking for extended periods of time are a way for the dog to relieve the stress.

• Lick granulomas can occur as a result of allergies. For example, allergic inhalant dermatitis creates stress in the skin resulting in inflammation and itching, which triggers the dog to lick at any convenient area. In this case, treatment for the allergy is often successful. It is a good idea to consider allergy testing in dogs with persistent lick granulomas or recurrent ones. With all itching skin conditions, also make sure all grooming equipment is kept scrupulously clean.

• Acral lick granulomas can occur secondary to injuries. For example, bone or joint pain can draw a dog's attention to the wrist or ankle area and in an attempt to alleviate the discomfort, the dog licks over the top of the joint.

• A foreign body such as a thistle spine or splinter might start up a reaction in the skin that draws the dog's attention to that particular spot.

• Hypothyroidism has played a role in some cases of acral lick granuloma. It is a good idea to have the thyroid gland function checked, especially in black labradors.

SYMPTOMS

• Thickened, oval, hairless red areas of skin.
• In some cases, the sores have ulcerated and oozing centres.
• The dog licks the area compulsively.

Make sure grooming tools are kept clean, and wear protective rubber gloves.

3

Clean lesions with an iodine-based product and wipe with alcohol to help dry out the affected area.

WHAT YOU AND YOUR VET CAN DO

• If an underlying cause cannot be found, then the lick granuloma is treated symptomatically. Topical treatment with antibiotic ointments, cortisone creams, and topical anaesthetic preparations help some dogs. Cortisone injections into and around the lesion shrinks the lesions temporarily, but affected dogs generally start licking again later.

• The psychological cases can respond to simple changes in lifestyle (reducing stress or preventing boredom). In more difficult cases, anti-anxiety drugs may be considered, whilst acupuncture works well in some dogs.

3

COMPLEMENTARY TREATMENTS

⊠ HERBAL REMEDIES

Try applying a solution of plantain (*Plantago major*) to the site. You can make this easily by adding the leaves of the plant to 250 ml (8 fl oz) of water. Boil the mixture for approximately five minutes, leave to stand for another five minutes and then sieve out the plant material. Apply the solution twice daily.

⊡ HOMEOPATHIC REMEDIES

Arsenica album 30c (one pellet every four hours) is helpful in cases of constant chewing and licking. Give one pellet every four hours for three treatments. Rescue Remedy (three drops, three to four times daily) helps calm the emotions.

Plantain leaves.

ALLERGIES

Allergic dermatitis is an inflammation of the skin that occurs after it has been exposed to an allergen. An allergen is something to which the body reacts badly. The number-one sign of allergies in pets is itching. Dogs lick, bite, chew and scratch themselves to the point of self-mutilation. The result is red, raw areas of skin with oozing sores and hair loss. The difficulty that vets face is isolating the allergen responsible for the reaction because there is often more than one substance involved.

TYPES OF ALLERGY

• Fleas cause over 50 percent of all allergies in dogs. The dogs are actually allergic to the flea saliva (see p. 44). The presence of just one flea on these dogs can cause intense itching that can lastfor up to two weeks.

• Atopy (allergic inhalant dermatitis), or atopic dermatitis, is the term used for allergies that develop in response to inhaled particles. Inhaled allergens, like housedust, mould and pollen, are the second most common type of allergy in dogs. These allergies start at a younger age in dogs and some breeds seem to be more prone, such as west highland white terriers and shar peis.

•Allergies to food occasionally occur in dogs (see p. 34). Trials of special hypoallergenic diets can be used to diagnose the offending dietary ingredients.

• Bacterial skin infections or pyodermas (see p. 56) are the most common complication of allergic skin disorders.

Discovering the source of an allergy is often a process of elimination. Your dog's bedding may be the culprit.

WHAT YOUR VET CAN DO

• Skin testing is the most accurate way to find out what your dog is allergic to. Small amounts of different substances (allergens) are injected under the skin. If the dog is allergic to one of the substances, the skin reacts by getting red and swollen at the site of the injection within 15 to 30 minutes. Once you know what the dog is allergic to, you then have to work out how to avoid it.

• With a suspected dietary allergy, your vet will probably advise you to place your dog on an elimination diet (see p. 34), for up to 12 weeks. Provide only water for the dog to drink, never milk, as this itself can cause an allergic reaction.

An elimination diet can be used to investigate food allergies.

• Hyposensitization, which makes a dog less sensitive to an allergen, is the best treatment option for allergies to such things as pollen and mould that are difficult to avoid. The dog is given "allergy shots", injections of small amounts of the actual allergen, weekly over a period of time. By increasing the amount gradually, the aim is to try to stimulate the body to become immune or less sensitive to the allergen.

3

• Cortisone and antihistamines can help reduce itching, and antibiotics can be used to treat secondary bacterial infection. Bathing with hypoallergenic oatmeal-based shampoos and leave-on after-shampoo moisturizers with aloe vera and alpha keri help decrease skin irritation. Omega 3 and 6 fatty acid supplements, zinc, along with antioxidant vitamins A, C, and E help dry flaky skin and haircoats.

• For ongoing flea problems, monthly flea products available through your vet are the safest and most effective way to prevent flea infestations (see p. 44).

COMPLEMENTARY TREATMENTS

☐ HOMEOPATHIC REMEDIES
A range of homeopathic remedies, of 30c to 1m, *Sulphur, Hepar sulph, Arsenicum alb*, and *Rhus tox*.

☒ HERBAL REMEDIES
Chinese herbal formulas that may be helpful are *Scutellaria, Tribulus, Anemarrhena* and *Capillaris*.

Acupuncture can stimulate the immune system and decrease the itching and inflammation.

BACTERIAL INFECTIONS

Bacterial skin infections are a major cause of itching in dogs. Most bacterial skin infections occur when the body's immune system is compromised by allergies, illness or stress. The medical term that is used for bacterial infections of the skin is "pyoderma", which literally means "pus in skin".

TYPES OF BACTERIAL INFECTION

• Staphylococcus ("staph") bacteria are the most common organisms found in bacterial skin disease in dogs. Small numbers of these bacteria normally live on intact skin in harmony, but when the outer protective layer of skin is abraded because of itching, these bacteria multiply and cause infection. Common signs include itchy red raw bumps, scabs and pustules. Later dry crusty areas of hair loss with an off-odour develop. The main area affected generally depends on the underlying cause. For example, bacterial infections secondary to flea allergies cause lesions over the back and near the tail. With inhalant allergies, face, feet, chin and abdomen are affected.

• Bacteria can also infect the skin between the toes. This is called interdigital pyoderma and often occurs with demodectic mange (see p. 46).

• Bacterial infections of the chin are called canine acne. Obese dogs and breeds with pushed-in faces have extra skin folds that often become infected. The skin here rubs together and is dark and damp, providing an ideal environment for bacteria to multiply.

The face, lips and vulva are the most common sites of skin folds where bacteria may multiply.

WHAT YOUR VET CAN DO

Inherited skin folds are an attractive feature of dogs like the shar pei.

• Antibiotics given by mouth for two to three weeks are effective for most bacterial skin infections. Small lesions can be treated topically. Bathing with benzol peroxide-type products is best for generalized infections. Alcohol wipes and unscented baby powder help dry out moist skin folds and infections.

• In severe cases corrective surgery can eliminate areas of excessive skin. Hyposensitization injections (see p. 55) with staphyloccocus vaccines are a very effective alternative to long-term antibiotics, especially for dogs with allergies that develop recurrent bacterial skin infections.

COMPLEMENTARY TREATMENTS

⊠ HERBAL REMEDIES
Adding goldenseal root tea to the daily diet is helpful for staph infections. Calendula lotion may be applied topically to a septic infection.

▣ HOMEOPATHIC REMEDIES
Hepar Sulphins may be beneficial when pus is present. *Sulphur* 30c is often recommended for treating bacterial skin infections.

SUNBURN

Excessive exposure to sunlight not only causes painful sunburn, it also increases the risk of skin cancer. Parts of the dog that are at highest risk are those where there is no hair or pigmentation, or where the skin is fair such as the underbelly, groin, and the inside of the hind legs. In areas well above sea level where ultraviolet (UV) light is especially strong, dogs like pointers, bull terriers, and dalmatians are often affected with skin cancer.

WHAT YOU CAN DO

• The obvious thing to do is prevent your dog from staying outdoors when the sun is at its hottest, from about 10 o'clock in the morning until the late afternoon.

• You can also apply a sunscreen to vulnerable parts of the body, notably those that have a relatively thin covering of hair. Use a cream with a Sun Protection Factor (SPF) greater than 30 and rub it in well. It is likely that your dog will try to lick the cream off, so avoid sunscreens that contain zinc or PABA (para-aminobenzoic acid), which could be harmful to your dog. Ask your vet or a pet shop to advise on the best products.

• Affected areas of skin become very red, painful and irritated. Soothe inflamed skin with cool water or cloths wrung out in cold water to help reduce the pain and discomfort.

Warning

Allowing your dog to become sunburned, especially on a regular basis, will greatly increase the risk of skin tumours forming in the future, especially the type known as squamous cell carcinomas.

Mexican hairless dog

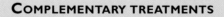

COMPLEMENTARY TREATMENTS

✕ HERBAL REMEDIES
If sunburned, the skin will be dry, so rub in a moisturizer such as jojoba or an aloe vera product, or apply hypericum lotion.

☐ HOMEOPATHIC REMEDIES
Use *Cantharis* if sores are present from sunburn.

Aloe vera

TUMOURS

A tumour is the result of an uncontrolled overgrowth of cells and it can be benign if the cell growth is restricted to a local area, like a mole. However, a malignant tumour (cancer) occurs when the cell growth is invasive. This can spread throughout the body and is capable of causing death. Any lump or bump you find on your dog should be examined by your vet as soon as possible. Lumps that grow fast, change size or shape, ooze or break open, are hard or are firmly attached to the body or have an unusual color are all cause for concern.

WHAT YOUR VET CAN DO

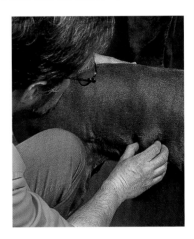

• Your vet can use a needle to withdraw some of the cells from a lump which can be examined under the microscope to tell if a lump is benign or malignant. If malignant, the vet might do a biopsy. A small piece of tissue is removed and examined under the microscope to confirm the diagnosis once the exact type of cancer is known. The most appropriate treatment can then be determined. Benign tumours should be monitored once or twice a year because occasionally they can become malignant.

3

• Cancer specialists (veterinary oncologists) offer treatment options for pets similar to those available for people. Treatment options are surgery, chemotherapy, and radiation therapy. New treatments include phototherapy, hyperthermia, cryosurgery, and immunotherapy (drug therapy to stimulate the immune system). The best treatment will depend on the type of tumour, extent of its development and the health status of the dog. If a cancerous tumour is discovered early, treatment options are greater, as is the chance of recovery.

COMPLEMENTARY TREATMENTS

⊠HERBAL REMEDIES
Herbal immune stimulation is often used in conjunction with conventional therapy.

Therapeutic nutrition includes "cancer-fighting diets" (low carbohydrates, increased fats and quality proteins). While such diet programmes may not appropriate for every pet or family, they may help to keep your pet happy and minimize discomfort in its remaining months.

CLAW PROBLEMS

Pedicures for pets are important because overgrown nails can cause painful infections. Some dogs are active enough to wear their toenails down, but if you can hear a clicking noise when your dog walks across a hard floor, its nails are probably too long. For most dogs, nail trims once a month are best. Many dogs do not like having their feet handled, but if you start trimming your dog's nails while it is still a puppy it might get more used to it.

A dew claw is a "fifth" toe located in the thumb position, which may or may not be present. If your dog has dew claws then they need trimming too. When dew claws overgrow they curl inward and can grow into the skin which can cause painful infections. They are also easily snagged, torn, and injured.

3

Regular clipping is important, not only for keeping the claws trim, but also to check for infection at the base of the claw.

WHAT YOU AND YOUR VET CAN DO

• Scissors should never be used for cutting the claws, simply because they are not strong enough for the task and may cause the nail to split, rather than cut cleanly. Use a nail clipper designed specifically for dogs, which can also be used for dew claws. Different styles are available commercially and work well as long as the blades are sharp. A metal nail file helps smooth edges down.

• A blood vessel runs down the centre of each nail that will bleed if it is cut too short. The vessel is easier to see on the white nails. Start with a white nail and use it as a reference for the dark nails. Just trim the tip that curves downward so the nail remains parallel to the toe.

• In case you trim a nail too short, have a styptic pencil (the one sold to stem shaving cuts) or silver nitrate stick on hand to stop the bleeding. Flour, cornflour or baking powder along with pressure will also work in an emergency.

• Each nail also contains a nerve (the quick). If you hit the nerve it really hurts. Professional groomers often use electric nail grinders that allow the quick to recede, resulting in a shorter nail and tighter paw.

• It's a good idea to check the dog's foot pads and trim excess hair between the toes.

• It is possible to have dew claws removed when the puppy is a few days old. Your vet can also take them off at six to nine months, at the same time as neutering your dog.

• If your dog is nervous, it might be better to ask the vet or a professional groomer to give your pet a nail trim.

Warning

Always keep a watch on your dog's claws as part of its regular grooming routine, because on occasions, an infection can develop at the base of the claw. The affected area will be swollen and painful – beware of trying to touch it because you may be bitten for your trouble. Instead seek veterinary advice. It may well be necessary to sedate your dog so that a thorough examination of the affected area can be carried out. Regular saltwater footbaths may then be required as part of the treatment process.

3

Guillotine clippers are much stronger than scissors and cut claws cleanly.

INTERDIGITAL PROBLEMS

The skin between the toes and between the foot pads—and less often the foot pads themselves—can be irritated or inflamed by a variety of problems. These include allergies, especially allergic inhalant dermatitis (see p. 54); dogs suffering from this will lick their feet excessively, which causes a rust-coloured discoloration to the feet. External irritants are another problem, for instance walking on lawn chemicals, herbicides, rug shampoos, pebbles, or hot road tar. Skin may also be irritated by infections, including generalized demodectic mange (see p. 46), bacteria (see p. 56) and fungal infections like yeast.

Another skin disease, pemphigus, may attack the foot pads, as well as the bridge of the nose, and the eyes. In this disease the body's immune system attacks itself for some unknown reason and affected dogs may have secondary bacterial infections and pus-filled sores which break open and form crusts.

3

WHAT YOU AND YOUR VET CAN DO

• Epsom salt soaks are soothing for the feet. Cotton socks can be helpful to protect sore feet.

• Spritz the dog's feet with water if dog is exposed to irritants in winter. Keep a spritzer bottle handy by the door and use it every time the dog comes inside. Dry the feet off immediately, particularly between the toes.

• Trim excess fur between toes and remove any mats in the hair between the foot pads.

• Diagnosis of pemphigus is by signs, lesion location, and biopsy. There is no cure so treatment is geared to symptomatic relief of foot lesions, antibiotics for secondary infection, and immune system stimulation.

SYMPTOMS

• Constant licking and chewing of the paws.
• Saliva from constant licking turns white feet a copper colour.

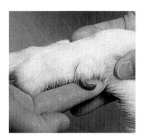

COMPLEMENTARY TREATMENTS

⬛ HERBAL REMEDIES
Ground up pumpkin seeds added to the diet are a good source of zinc and help cases of pemphigus.

⬛ HOMEOPATHIC REMEDIES
Sulphur 30c should bring relief in cases of external irritants when given twice daily.

SYSTEMIC ILLNESSES

Systemic illness is defined as a disease of any major organ system or any condition that ultimately affects the entire body. The signs will vary depending on which organ is involved—for instance the heart, liver, or kidney. The keys to making sure your dog has the highest possible quality and length of life are early recognition and reduction of predisposing health risk factors, as well as an accurate diagnosis and prompt correction. The more observant you are, the easier it will be to work with your vet to ensure your dog's optimal health.

4

YOUR DOG'S HEALTH

When you first become the owner of a new dog, it is a good idea to have it checked over by a vet. While there are certain things about your pet that you will know, there can be underlying medical conditions that can be diagnosed only by a proper clinical examination. For a puppy, you should also start a course of vaccines, to give it the best chance of a full and healthy life.

VACCINES AND NOSODES

• Vaccines (shots) help protect your dog against many of the most serious and potentially fatal diseases caused by bacteria and viruses. Since dogs are most susceptible to infections as puppies, vaccines begin at six weeks and are given at three to four week intervals until the puppy is 16 weeks old. After that, it's just once a year. The most important vaccines are for infectious canine distemper, infectious canine hepatitis, leptospirosis, parainfluenza, parvovirus, coronavirus, rabies (where appropriate), kennel cough and Lyme disease. Once vaccinated against a particular disease, if the dog is later exposed to that disease, it will either not be affected at all or it may have a mild case of the disease from which it will recover.

4

• Homeopathic vaccines are called nosodes. Nosodes are made from natural disease products. They are sterilized, diluted, and prepared so that they are safe and efficacious. Nosodes are given by mouth over a period of time that may extend from weeks to months.

All dogs are susceptible to congential and inherited diseases. Certain pedigrees are at higher risk than others, so a clinical examination by your vet is important.

TIPS FOR YOUR DOG'S GOLDEN YEARS

• People and pets are both living longer now than ever before. Dogs become senior citizens at the age of eight and, just like people, have special needs. To improve the quality of your senior dog's life, feed a high-quality diet specifically formulated for your pet's age and lifestyle. Cut calories by 30 per cent, decrease fat and protein and increase the fibre to provide enough bulk so your dog feels full. Moderate exercise of at least 20 minutes a day is good for the heart and lungs and it also increases muscle tone.

• Latest treatments for senior dogs reap the benefit of human experience. They include veterinary dental care for periodontal disease, which is a leading cause of heart disease; and new medications for arthritis and for Alzheimer's disease, which has now been diagnosed as a syndrome affecting dogs (see p. 83).

AGE AND SIZE

There is actually a natural variance in the lifespan of dogs, divided not so much on the basis of the different breeds, but rather in terms of size. Large dogs have a short potential lifespan, living little more than a decade in most cases, whereas smaller ones may live well into their teens.

4

CARDIOVASCULAR DISEASE

Well over three million dogs have some form of acquired heart disease and may be in heart failure. Heart failure results from the heart's inability to pump blood at a rate necessary to meet the body's needs. As the heart works harder, further heart damage occurs.

HEART FAILURE

Two forms of heart disease occur in dogs: dilated cardiomyopathy (DCM) and mitral valve insufficiency (MVI). In dilated cardiomyopathy the muscle of the heart's wall gets thin and weak so that it can't contract properly and circulation is impaired. In mitral valve insufficiency the heart valve fibres degenerate and cannot close correctly, so blood flow and circulation are affected. Cardiomyopathy is common in large breeds, like great Danes, whereas valve disease often occurs in older small breeds, such as miniature poodles and dachshunds. Signs of heart failure include getting tired easily; coughing, especially when waking up in the morning; difficulty breathing; fainting; weakness; and lack of energy.

THE CIRCULATORY SYSTEM

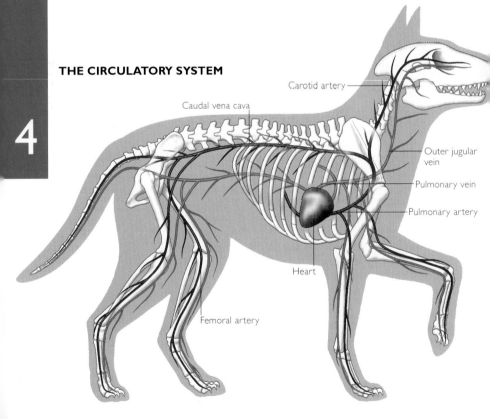

Carotid artery

Caudal vena cava

4

Outer jugular vein

Pulmonary vein

Pulmonary artery

Heart

Femoral artery

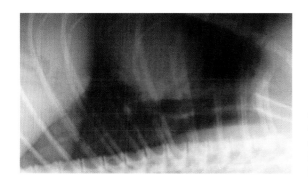

A chest X ray can reveal certain tell-tale signs of a cardiac condition. The heart is the faint circular shape in the middle of the picture.

WHAT YOUR VET CAN DO

• To diagnose heart disease your vet will give your dog a physical examination. It will include listening to the heart with a stethoscope, taking chest X rays, and doing an electrocardiograph (ECG), which detects electrical disturbances in the heart. An echocardiograph may also be recommended, which lets your vet see into the dog's heart. It works like an ultrasound machine and helps determine if valve problems exist.

• Depending on the form of heart disease, treatment may include one or all of the "four Ds" of heart failure therapy: a diet of low sodium; diuretics to reduce fluid build-up and help kidneys eliminate excess sodium and water; dilators, which are drugs to help dilate or enlarge veins to allow blood to flow more easily; and digoxin (digitalis), which is a drug to help the heart beat stronger and more slowly, so increasing its efficiency.

• Pacemaker surgery is an effective treatment for electrical disturbances in the heart in some dogs that are unresponsive to medical management. These are dogs that faint, have a slow heart rate, and tire easily with exercise. The pacemaker is inserted into the jugular vein and placed down into the heart. The wires are attached to a pulse generator which is placed under the skin of the neck. The pacemaker lasts for the dog's entire life. Owners need to use a harness instead of a collar post-operatively because of the location of the generator in the dog's neck.

4

COMPLEMENTARY TREATMENTS

🗀 HOMEOPATHIC REMEDIES

Crataegus oxycantha 3x (hawthorne berry) is helpful for heart weakness and heart murmurs: one pellet on the tongue once daily for four weeks. Allow no food 10 minutes before or after treatment.

Digitalis purpurea 6x (foxglove) smoothes irregularities: one tablet if the dog has a fainting attack and blue tongue following exertion. *Cactus grandiflorus* 6c is recommended when there are circulatory problems and the heart valves are leaking.

ENDOCRINE DISORDERS

The endocrine system is made up of seven glands that send hormones in the blood to other parts of the body in order to stimulate a response. Each gland deals with a different function. Whenever there is either a lower (referred to as "hypo") or higher (referred to as "hyper") hormonal output than necessary, symptoms of illness are likely to become apparent. The thyroid glands in the neck, which regulate the body's metabolism and growth, and the pancreas, close to the small intestine, which controls the sugar level in the blood, are most significant in relation to your dog's health. The parathyroid glands, near the thyroid, control calcium production and the adrenal glands produce cortisol and adrenaline—the "flight or fight" hormone required in stressful situations.

COMMON ENDOCRINE DISORDERS

• Diabetes mellitus (also known as sugar diabetes) is the most common hormonal disorder in dogs. A lack of the hormone insulin means that sugar (blood glucose) stays in the blood stream and is lost into the urine, so the body's cells cannot get nourishment. Middle-aged overweight female dogs are most often affected. Initial signs of diabetes are excess eating, drinking and urinating. Weeks to months later cataracts may develop because the eyes have been deprived of nutrients. Left untreated, vomiting, depression and loss of appetite also occur.

4

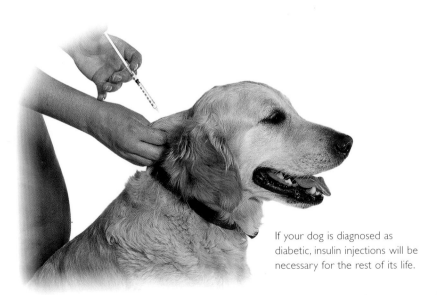

If your dog is diagnosed as diabetic, insulin injections will be necessary for the rest of its life.

• The thyroid gland produces the hormone that controls the metabolic rate. If the gland does not produce enough, hypothyroidism is the result. Often the cause is unknown, but occasionally the body's immune system destroys the gland. Signs of hypothyroidism include hair loss (evenly distributed on each side of the dog and without itching); weight gain, without an increase in appetite; lethargy; dry flaky skin; and ear infections. The signs develop slowly over several months to a year.

• Overproduction of cortisol by the adrenal glands causes Cushing's disease, characterized by a greatly increased thirst and corresponding output of urine. Abdominal distention becomes common in the latter stages.

• Underproduction of cortisol by the adrenal glands results in Addison's disease. Signs are quite general and often include vomiting, diarrhoea and increasing weakness.

WHAT YOU AND YOUR VET CAN DO

• Diagnosis of diabetes includes blood and urine tests which both show elevated blood sugar levels. There is no cure, but insulin replacement is an effective control. Insulin requirements can change and must be monitored daily for life; too much insulin can cause life-threatening seizures.

• To keep insulin requirements consistent, a low-carbohydrate, low-fat, high-fibre diet must be given 30 minutes before each injection. Meals must be given twice a day at the same time and snacks avoided. Exercise should remain consistent. Dogs should be neutered because reproductive cycles can alter insulin requirements. Since diabetes also has an hereditary link, neutering also helps prevent transmission to future generations. Properly regulated diabetic dogs can lead long healthy lives, but their owners must be prepared to make a serious committment to the treatment.

• Diagnosis of hypothyroidism is made by a blood test that detects decreased levels of thyroid hormone. Whilst thyroid disease is not curable, it can be controlled with oral thyroid hormone replacement, which is safe, effective, and relatively inexpensive. Lifelong replacement is generally needed, but most owners are pleasantly surprised to see their old dog rejuvenated after 8–12 weeks. Hair regrows, body weight decreases, and ear problems clear up.

4

COMPLEMENTARY TREATMENTS

☒ HERBAL REMEDIES

Kelp stimulates the thyroid gland: give the dog 1.25 ml (1/4 tsp) daily. Raw green vegetables help to lower blood sugar levels.

Raw broccoli and cabbage

☐ HOMEOPATHIC REMEDIES

Phosphorus 6x (one pellet on the tongue once daily for four weeks) can help dogs suffering from sugar diabetes. For dogs with hypothyroidism, try Nux vomica 30c daily for five days.

KIDNEY PROBLEMS

The kidneys serve many vital functions. They filter and remove toxic waste from the body via the urine, regulate calcium and vitamin D levels, maintain the amount of fluid in the body, and secrete the hormone responsible for red blood cell production. Any process that interferes with the kidneys' ability to function properly can cause kidney disease, which is the second leading cause of death in dogs. In most cases, progressive age-related deterioration of the kidneys is responsible, with no apparent cause.

Other causes of kidney disease include bacterial and viral infections, nutritional factors, an immune system defect, toxins, or inherited breed defects.

Acute kidney disease occurs suddenly and is rare in dogs, but with prompt treatment it is generally reversible. Chronic kidney disease (called chronic renal disease, or CRD) is the most common situation and occurs when the kidneys deteriorate slowly over several years. CRD is not reversible.

SYMPTOMS

- Increased thirst and urinary output are characteristic of chronic renal failure, with the damaged kidneys no longer being able to produce a concentrated urine. Tests to exclude other conditions with similar symptoms (such as diabetes mellitus, Cushing's disease and urinary tract problems) will be necessary.
- Loss of weight, depression, loss of appetite and occasional vomiting occur because of the build-up of ammonia in the blood.
- Signs of chronic kidney disease generally do not occur until 80 percent of the kidney function is lost.

4

THE KIDNEYS

Kidneys

Bladder

WHAT YOUR VET CAN DO

• The vet will diagnose the cause of urinary incontinence by a physical examination, blood and urine tests, and X rays of the abdomen.

• For oestrogen-responsive urinary incontinence, oestrogen replacement therapy is very effective. Tablets are given daily and the problem usually resolves itself in less than a week.

• In some cases surgery may be the only way to remove bladder stones. In others, a special diet can dissolve the stones; it works by reducing the excess of minerals which form the stones.

Warning

Urolithiasis is a disease caused by the presence and effects of stones (called uroliths) or crystals (called calculi) in the urinary tract. Stones can block the urine flow, prevent elimination of poisonous waste, and are potentially fatal. The vet will have to correct the blockage and empty the dog's bladder. A diet to prevent stones forming will be recommended following treatment: up to 50 percent of treated cases recur if preventive measures are not taken.

4

COMPLEMENTARY TREATMENTS

⊠ HERBAL REMEDIES
Shepherd's purse (*Thlaspi bursa pastoris*) will usually bring some relief.

⊡ HOMEOPATHIC REMEDIES
Belladonna 30c may be recommended for sudden urinary infections, particularly where the urine is dark in colour. *Urtica urens* 3x will encourage urinary flow, lessening the risk of kidney stones forming, while *Hydrangea* 3x is a useful preventive in this respect.

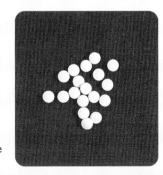

REPRODUCTIVE PROBLEMS

Most male and female dogs are mature enough to reproduce between the ages of six and nine months onward. Female dogs generally go through an oestrus or heat cycle every six months, in spring and autumn. Several days prior to the true heat cycle the female dog goes through a bleeding cycle, when she is very receptive to male dogs. Personality changes in female dogs include becoming short-tempered and anxious. Surgical neutering of female dogs eliminates all heat cycles, bleeding and personality changes.

PYOMETRA

Pyometra is a potentially life-threatening infection of the uterus that occurs in middle-aged female dogs that are not spayed. The hormone progesterone causes the walls of the uterus to thicken and the cervix to close. This creates a suitable environment in which bacteria can grow. They multiply slowly for several years and eventually the uterus fills with pus and the dog becomes sick.

There are two types of pyometra, depending on whether the cervix is open or closed. Open pyometra occurs during or just after the heat cycle when the cervix is still open. Since the cervix is open, the pus, along with the blood-tinged or clear fluid, exits through the vulva. You will see or smell the foul vaginal discharge and the dog will have a slight fever, be lethargic, thirsty and may vomit. Closed pyometra occurs one to three months after the heat cycle when the dog's cervix is closed. Pus cannot drain out of the body, so it stays in the uterus and some of the bacteria from the uterus enter the bloodstream. This can lead to a blood infection called septicaemia which can quickly be fatal. Signs include a high fever, weakness, lack of appetite, and vomiting.

4

A sudden attachment to an object, such as a toy, can be a symptom of false pregnancy.

Warning

In the case of male dogs, it is important to ensure that both testes descend into the scrotum, because if retained within the abdomen, they are likely to cause a Sertoli cell tumour. They should usually have descended by the age of six months. Small breeds, such as Yorkshire terriers, are most vulnerable to retained testicles.

WHAT YOUR VET CAN DO

• The treatment of choice for pyometra has been to remove the infected uterus and ovaries, usually a surgical emergency to save the dog's life. Dogs with pyometra are often in shock, dehydrated, and have concurrent kidney failure. Vets often have to decide whether the treatment or the disease is the most life-threatening. Once a dog has been affected with pyometra, recurrence is common, so most dogs with either type are spayed.

• Extremely valuable breeding bitches with the open cervix type of pyometra have a new option for medical treatment with a hormone called prostaglandin F2 alpha. This hormone causes the uterus to contract and expel the pus.

• Spaying and neutering dogs is also an important part of responsible pet ownership. It helps reduce overpopulation and decreases the number of unwanted dogs that end up in shelters or are euthanized. Female neutering involves removal of the ovaries, fallopian tubes, and uterus. Spaying before the first heat cycle at six months of age dramatically decreases the risk of mammary and uterine cancer and eliminates pyometra that can develop later in life.

• Neutering male dogs involves surgical removal of the testicles, so testicular cancer is virtually eliminated. It also decreases urine odour and territorial urine marking. Neutered male dogs are less likely to roam and are generally happy to stay at home. Its personality will not change, although aggressive tendencies are reduced.

4

COMPLEMENTARY TREATMENTS

☐ HOMEOPATHIC REMEDIES

In the case of pyometra, using *Caulophyllum* 30c may help to improve the bitch's condition prior to surgery, especially when the pyometra is open and discharging.

Sepia 30c (cuttlefish) is also often recommended in cases of pyometra.

The treatment usually involves giving one tablet three times during the day, at four-hourly intervals.

EPILEPSY

The main sign of epilepsy is seizures. These are caused by abnormal electrical activity that begins in the brain. Most seizures last from one to three minutes, with the average time being 90 seconds. Minor (partial motor) seizures can cause dogs to salivate, stare into space, or have localized muscle twitches. Severe (grand mal) seizures can cause dogs to lose control totally. Afterward, some dogs act normally, others remain dazed. Seizures burn up a lot of energy so most dogs are hungry and will want to eat after an epileptic episode.

Some cases of epilepsy in dogs occur as a result of diseases such as diabetes, kidney failure, and brain tumours. Those dogs are usually over six years old before they start having seizures. However, most cases of epilepsy in dogs are termed "idiopathic"—meaning that the cause is unknown. Classically the onset is between one and five years of age, with a higher incidence in certain breeds, such as golden retrievers, cocker spaniels, huskies, malamutes, and miniature poodles.

WHAT YOU AND YOUR VET CAN DO

• All dogs that suffer from seizures should be checked by a vet. The vet will do a physical examination along with blood tests, a urinalysis and X rays. If an underlying problem can be found (e.g. diabetes or kidney disease) it can be treated and the seizures may stop. In dogs with idiopathic epilepsy, no underlying problem can be found, so only control rather than cure is possible.

SYMPTOMS

• Salivation.
• Paddles on its side.
• Pupils are dilated.
• May act dazed.
• May lose urine or bowel control.

4

• Various anticonvulsant medications are usually prescribed. Daily medications are not recommended unless the dog suffers seizures more than once a month. With proper treatment most epileptic dogs are able to lead normal lives that are only slightly shorter than normal.

COMPLEMENTARY TREATMENTS

☐ HOMEOPATHIC REMEDIES

Silicea 30c (silicon dioxide) can be helpful: one dose of two whole pellets or three pellets crushed to a powder on the tongue. Allow no food one hour before or after. Wait for a month, then reassess the condition. Many owners also find acupuncture useful for controlling epilepsy in dogs.

BEHAVIOURAL PROBLEMS

Proper play promotes socialization and a well-socialized puppy makes a great pet. Begin the process as soon as your puppy comes home, ideally at eight weeks. That's the best time for puppies to bond with people. From eight to ten weeks puppies are impressionable and need to have as many positive experiences with people and other animals as possible. Ten to 16 weeks is the time for puppies to learn. It should be fun. Your puppy should learn through positive reinforcement. Don't use punishments, but instead withold rewards. Use common sense and judgement, just as you would with a child.

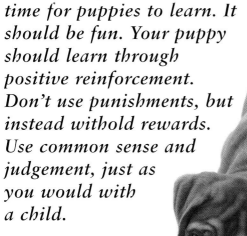

TRAINING

Training is basic obedience. It's teaching your dog to sit, stay, come, and heel. When your dog learns to listen to you, then you can do lots of fun things together. Best results are achieved from training between eight weeks and seven months.

TRAINING YOUR DOG

The best way to start training is with positive reinforcement. Try to work out what your puppy likes best (food, a particular toy, or physical affection), and use that as the reward when it performs the correct behaviour for you. Turn favourite activities into games. Based on natural instincts, certain breeds enjoy certain games. For example, springers like to run, so throw them a ball. Creative game educate your puppy and provide a physical outlet for all that energy. They also promote emotional and social growth, improve coordination, and enhance your relationship.

Avoid rough games like tug-of-war, wrestling and chasing because they teach your puppy to struggle against you.

WHAT YOU AND YOUR VET CAN DO

- Even the best trained dogs only listen 80 percent of the time, so when your puppy doesn't listen, be patient and don't give up. If your puppy is doing something dangerous, then use negative reinforcement to stop it right away so it doesn't hurt itself. For example, to deter it from chewing on an electric cord, spray your puppy with water or make a sudden loud noise.

- If you do encounter a behavioural worry with your dog at any stage, it is important to seek assistance without delay. Discuss the problem with your vet, who can check for any underlying medical condition that could be responsible for unexpected changes in behaviour. The vet can also refer you to a behavioural specialist.

5

• Older dogs that chew excessively may have either a medical or behavioural problem. First check with your vet: have a complete physical and dental examination. The vast majority of dogs over eight years old have peridontal disease, along with painful gums and gingivitis. A professional dental cleaning should alleviate this problem (see p. 17).

PUPPY-PROOFING YOUR HOME

• When you bring home a new puppy, expect to adjust your lifestyle, expect inconvenience, and plant to spend a lot of time with your puppy, especially in the beginning. Make your house and garden as safe as possible. Puppies are just like toddlers—everything they see goes into their mouth. So look at your house from a puppy's perspective. Crawl around on your hands and knees if you need to. Look for temptations that could be dangerous like electric cords, small objects they can chew up, swallow, and choke on like toys, and plants that might be poisonous like holly, ivy, and azaleas. Outside, be careful where you put pesticides (e.g. ant killer, rat poison) and antifreeze containers. Be sure your garbage bin is out of reach and has a secure lid.

• If you see your puppy doing something dangerous, use negative reinforcement to stop it right away so it does not hurt itself. So, for example, if you see it chewing on an electric cord, make a sudden loud noise. Use a shake can: fill an empty drinks can with a handful of pennies (they fit right through the slot) and start shaking.

KEEPING YOUR PUPPY BUSY

Toys help keep puppies from becoming bored and chewing on household items like your furniture. Toys also stimulate your puppy's mind and encourage problem solving. Talking toys and educational toys are instant boredom busters. Other toys can be stuffed with peanut butter or cheese. Certain cube-type toys are divided up into compartments so you can load them up with dry food or treats. As the puppy pushes the cube the treats are released to keep its interest and reward its efforts.

A selection of toys will help divert your dog's attention away from your shoes and furniture.

5

HOUSETRAINING

Good housetraining techniques teach your dog to relieve itself where and when you'd like it to. Dogs instinctively mark their own territory. Therefore, your goal is to teach your dog the boundaries of its territory. Housetraining can be learned in four to eight weeks and can start when your puppy is eight weeks old.

WHAT YOU CAN DO

• First of all, buy a crate. Be sure it's the right size: it should be large enough for comfort, but not too big otherwise the puppy will sleep at one end and use the other end for its business. If you get an airline-approved one, you can use it to travel, like a mobile home. You may be able to find a crate with an adjustable divider and slide the divider back as your puppy grows.

• Puppies need to go outside when they wake up, after every meal, and before bedtime. Most puppies eliminate within the first hour after eating. They should be fed two to three times each day, at the same time. Food should be left out for 20 to 30 minutes, then removed, and the last meal should be finished five hours before bedtime.

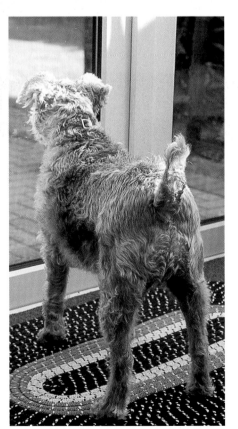

• Take the puppy out on a leash through the same door to the same spot every time, and when it does its business, reward with praise. If your puppy does not eliminate when you take it outside, bring it inside, put it in its crate for 15 minutes, and repeat the procedure until you achieve success. This time when you bring it in don't put it back in its crate. Confine your puppy to a relatively small, safe area of your home and provide constant supervision until your puppy is housetrained.

• If you have to leave your puppy at home alone each day for long periods, restrict it to a larger area such as a small room or exercise pen. This area should have enough space for sleeping and eating. Several feet away, place paper where elimination is to be.

5

• A common mistake is to let your dog go outside alone. Many dogs come back inside the house and then do their business. This causes most people to become upset. Their reaction inadvertently reinforces a negative behaviour. If your dog relieves itself in front of you, softly tell a shy dog "no", or use a firmer tone with a stubborn dog. Then take it to the spot on a leash where it is supposed to relieve itself and offer it immediate praise. Correcting your dog after the fact—even if it only happened a few minutes before—is ineffective because dogs have no way of associating your discipline with a past behaviour.

• If your puppy does make a mistake inside, its important to get rid of the odour. Effective products are available commercially and can be recommended by your vet. Using ammonia to clean up a mistake can actually make it worse and encourage the dog to return to the same place.

CANINE COGNITIVE DYSFUNCTION

• A lapse in toilet training can strike later in life. Canine cognitive dysfunction syndrome (CDS) is the equivalent of Alzheimer's disease in humans. It is the third leading reason for euthanasia by vets, and affects seven million dogs ten years of age and older. It is an age-related deterioration of cognitive abilities characterized by behavioural changes that include loss of house training, disorientation, aimless wandering, staring into space, decreased responsiveness to family members, confusion and excessive sleeping.

• There is no blood test or scan to test for cognitive dysfunction; the physical evidence can be found after the death. Vets make the diagnosis by ruling out other problems that cause similar symptoms. Anipryl is a one-a-day pill that has shown significant results: over 77 percent of dogs show marked improvement in less than 30 days with this new medication.

Warning

Deworming on a regular basis (see p. 39) is vital to eliminate the risk of *Toxocara* roundworms being spread to people, especially children. The eggs may be passed in puppies' faeces.

5

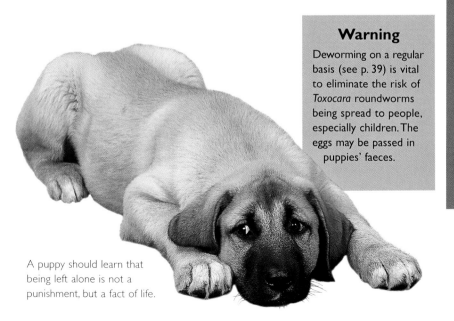

A puppy should learn that being left alone is not a punishment, but a fact of life.

SEPARATION ANXIETY

Canine separation anxiety is a complex behavioural disorder that occurs in response to separation from the person to whom the dog is most attached. Dogs with this disorder are often well behaved when the owner or family is home, but when left alone they panic. Signs include destructive behaviour such as chewing and digging, inappropriate elimination, excessive salivation, as well as barking and whining. Fourteen percent of dogs suffer from it, and it is the second leading reason for owners requesting euthanasia.

WHAT YOU CAN DO

• A way to be sure whether or not your dog suffers form separation anxiety is to videotape it when you leave. There are other disorders and illnesses with similar signs, so a consultation with your vet will help determine the problem.

Warning

When you leave a dog that suffers from canine separation anxiety, it can cause the dog severe anxiety. The dog may start to panic as it sees you getting ready to go out. Try to give your dog clear departure clues, like putting on your coat, playing with your car keys, at times other than when you are intending to leave. This will help your dog gradually to become indifferent to them.

5

• Dogs with separation anxiety cannot control their behaviour, and so should not be punished for it. Verbal reprimands and punishment can actually make your dog more anxious and make the problem worse. The addition of another dog usually does not help.

• Techniques to control canine separation anxiety include a programme of behavioural training that is simple and easy to follow. For instance, you might be told to avoid elaborate goodbyes (ignore your dog 30 minutes before you leave) and leave a special food-filled treat in your absence. When you come home, ignore your dog until it is quiet and relaxed. Avoid constant physical contact with it to encourage independence. Teach your dog to sit and stay in place, and praise its calm behaviour as you increase the distance between you, as well as the time spent being away. This helps it become independent and cope with being alone.

• As a complementary treatment, try Bach Flower Essence Rescue Remedy. Add it to the water bowl so that your dog has access to it all day.

WHAT YOUR VET CAN DO

• Separation anxiety is best controlled through a two-part plan that combines behavioural training with a daily medication called Clomicalm. Clomicalm helps relieve your dog's anxiety and makes it easier for it to learn new positive behaviours. At least 75 percent of dogs on this treatment show an improvement in less than 30 days. The length of treatment varies with the individual case.

• Acupuncture may be effective in some cases since it temporarily increases serotonin and dopamine levels in the brain.

5

Behaviour modification techniques establish a well balanced relationship between you and promote independence in your pet.

AGGRESSION

The purpose of training a puppy is to have a well-mannered pet. Training can also mean the difference between life and death. Bad behaviour is the number-one reason why owners have their dogs put to sleep—this is what happens to ten million dogs each year. Another statistic is that about one million people are treated for dog bites each year. Aggressive behaviour cannot be ignored. The longer it continues, the harder it is to change.

Warning

Even a good-natured dog can become aggressive under certain circumstances, most notably if it is in pain, so always handle a dog in this state with particular care to avoid being bitten.

WHY DOGS ARE AGGRESSIVE

• There are inherent differences in the level of aggression shown by various breeds. Traditionally, German shepherds, Rottweilers, Doberman pinschers, and pit bulls were considered aggressive, but statistics indicate that cocker spaniels and poodles are the main offenders.

• Aggressive behaviour can result from medical or psychological disorders. First, rule out medical problems with your vet, like separation anxiety (see p. 84) or cognitive dysfunction syndrome (see p. 83). Veterinary behaviourists are best suited to deal with psychological disorders since mishandled aggression can potentially be dangerous.

WHAT YOUR VET CAN DO

• If your dog bites you unexpectedly, it is advisable to seek veterinary advice. There could be an underlying medical problem, pain from problems such as arthritic hips or infected ears, or, in rare cases, an apparent inherited quirk that causes the dog to become transiently aggressive. Such animals are a liability, and it is vital to diagnose this type of problem at the earliest opportunity.

5

WHAT YOU CAN DO

• Before you buy a dog, there are a few things to keep in mind. It is important to act responsibly and not to buy on impulse. Be honest with yourself about the amount of time and work you're willing and able to put into a dog. Remember that a dog can be a 15- to 20-year emotional commitment.

Warning

The great worry in many countries is that dogs may be infected by the viral illness called rabies. Rabies affects all warm-blooded animals, including humans and dogs. The virus is shed in the saliva and transmitted through a bite wound. Humans can be infected through the bite of an infected animal. The virus attacks the nerves, resulting in paralysis and death. All dogs should be vaccinated for rabies.

• If you have children, choose the breed of dog carefully, bearing in mind the temperament of the breed. In all cases, try to match the personality of the dog with the personality and lifestyle of yourself and your family. Don't choose the most aggressive puppy or the most timid one in the litter. Look at the whole litter, see how they act, and take to your heart the puppy that reacts to you. Once you've made your pick, it's time to begin socialization and training (see p. 78).

• Train your dog from a very young age to give up an item on command. Many cases of aggression stem from owners attempting to take objects away from dogs that have not learned this.

• If your dog becomes over-excited during the rough and tumble of a game, it may nip. Do not confuse this behaviour with aggression but you should stop the game, to calm things down.

• Dogs can be affected by the weather, just like you can. Studies have shown that they are far more likely to bite when the weather is humid and thundery. Take care that your pet is not under stress at such times.

5

THIEVING

Dogs can develop bad habits because of a lack of training or poor initial training. Behaviour that was permissible in a puppy is no longer acceptable when the dog is older. This may be the case with thievery, which may have been a fun game when puppies were young. But dogs can make themselves seriously ill if, for example, they manage to steal chocolate. This contains a chemical called theobromine, large quantities of which are toxic to the central nervous system. The lethal dose of theobromine depends on the size of dog and the type of chocolate—dark cooking chocolate, for example, has more theobromine than milk chocolate.

Chocolate is not good for dogs.

CAUSES

• Dogs can steal for a variety of reasons but in most cases they do it because it's fun. When your dog steals food from the kitchen worktop you chase it around the house and it thinks that's a lot of fun.

• In rare cases dogs steal food because they are hungry. This may occur in a dog that previously had good manners and suddenly begins to steal. If this dog is thin it either needs more meals, better quality food or it might have worms. Take it to the vet to be sure there are no other underlying health problems and check a stool sample to rule out worms.

WHAT YOU CAN DO

• Once you know the thieving is just bad behaviour, then it's time for a programme of behavioural modification to eliminate the bad habit. The solution is to set up a situation that is not fun. Use a negative reinforcement to cause an unpleasant result. In most cases, after a few times and regardless of the temptation, the item won't look good anymore.

• For the negative reinforcement you can use anything that startles the dog and is unpleasant. For example, blast with a horn or use a shake can (see p. 81). You could toss a water balloon or a large key ring. You can also taint the item with hot pepper sauce or a mix of equal parts of alcohol, lemon juice, and vinegar. It won't hurt your dog, it just tastes terrible. As an example: put some freshly cooked meat on the worktop and taint it with hot pepper sauce. When the dog takes it, it will be sorry.

5

• Never get into the habit of feeding your dog anything from the table. When you sit down to a meal, remove the dog from the room.

• Dogs, especially puppies, are curious and like to investigate. Be sure to put things away, well out of your pet's reach. You need to be particularly careful not to leave tempting food around the house.

Leaving unattended shopping in the house can present too much temptation for most dogs.

COPROPHAGIA

One particularly unpleasant habit associated with some dogs is coprophagia, when they eat their own faeces. It can be due to intestinal parasites (see p. 38) or a deficiency of various vitamins and minerals. Adult dogs with exocrine pancreatic insufficiency (EPI) eat their faeces because they are unable to digest properly or absorb the nutrients they need in their diet, so they become extremely hungry and lose weight rapidly. These dogs need blood and other tests to find the cause of the problem. Adult German shepherds are the prime victims. Always check with your vet any worrying signs in your dog and make sure you take your dog out on a leash and clean up promptly. You can also obtain a special product to mix with food that helps dogs with a bad habit.

5

BARKING

One of the traits of domestic dogs that distinguishes them from their wolf ancestors is their readiness to make their presence known by barking. In some circumstances it can be useful, a warning of the presence of an intruder, for example, but a neighbourhood dog that barks continuously will be regarded as a serious nuisance.

CAUSES

• Barking is normal behaviour for dogs. Some dogs bark to defend their territory, as a greeting, an invitation to play, or because they're happy. Other dogs bark as a threat, because they're lonely, do not have enough exercise, or are frightened by thunder or fireworks.

• Certain breeds are more vocal than others. For example, beagles bark a lot and greyhounds hardly ever make a sound. Smaller breeds, especially terriers, often prove to be the most noisy.

WHAT YOU CAN DO

• The first step in dealing with your dog's barking is to gain an understanding of what stimulates its excessive barking behaviour. Keep a note of when and where the problem seems most persistent.

• Since barking is normal behaviour, it is more realistic to try to reduce it rather than eliminating it. For example, try teaching your dog to bark on command, then teach it to be quiet on command, and release excess energy with exercise.

• Obedience training, using positive and negative reinforcement (see p. 78), is a good addition to any dog's life. Blowing a horn, shaking a can, dropping a water balloon or tossing a key ring can all be enough to divert its attention from barking. Be sure not to reward your dog in any way for barking inappropriately. Instead, praise it for being quiet. Remember, be consistent and practise your commands daily.

5

FIRST AID

To help ensure the health of your dog and your family, a few preventive measures and a lot of common sense are important. It's a good idea to have a first aid kit and learn a few basic first aid techniques. Keep a list of emergency phone numbers on hand, including that of your vet and a 24-hour care facility. Always consult your vet before giving medicine to your dog and never give it prescription or over-the-counter medications intended for people. If your dog has a chronic or ongoing health condition, keep a written record of all medications and notes on its condition. If you have any concerns about your dog's health, talk to your vet.

6

DANGERS IN THE HOME

Dogs can often end up in situations where they are in danger and sustain actual injury, requiring emergency assistance. Dangerous situations in the home include the presence of chemicals and live electrical wiring, for example. The garden may contain plants that pose risks to them, though reports of dogs becoming seriously ill from eating plants are relatively rare compared to reports of poisoning from household products or drugs.

POTENTIAL DANGERS

• Pet poisoning by household drugs is very common. It is responsible for 75 percent of toxin exposure and carries a 20 percent fatality rate. Aspirin and other human non-steroidal anti-inflammatory pain relievers (NSAIDs) can be toxic to dogs. Signs of severe poisoning include excess salivation, vomiting, and weakness.

• Many household chemicals can also be harmful if consumed by a dog. Most cleansing materials can cause stomach upset and vomiting if they are eaten. Dishwasher detergent can produce burns in the mouth.

• Dogs often vomit after chewing on plants, but only severe or persistent vomiting is a danger sign. The best advice is to always consult your vet if concerned. Poisonous plants, especially for puppies, include *Taxus* (Japanese yew), which contains a potentially fatal heart toxin that can cause sudden death from heart failure, and rhododendrons and deadly nightshade.

6

SYMPTOMS

- Severe vomiting, salivating and weakness are all signs of poisoning.
- Sudden difficulty in breathing may suggest a bone in the throat, or a collision with a vehicle if your dog has been out roaming. Shortness of breath can also occur in some cases of poisoning.
- Pawing at the mouth may suggest discomfort caused by eating something hot, a sting by an insect or an obstruction in the mouth.

WHAT YOU CAN DO

- Take care when using household chemicals, if necessary keeping your dog out of the room. Keep dogs away from fresh paint, varnish, or stains until these finishes have dried completely. Outside, keep a dog off a lawn treated with insecticide or a weed killer.

- Keep your home as safe as possible by storing medications for all family members and pets in high closed cabinets, out of reach.

Be aware of where your dog is. A wandering dog can easily get itself into danger, especially around water.

Warning

Many insecticides meant to kill fleas and ticks contain organophosphates and carbamates that are toxic to a dog's nervous system. Signs of toxicity include salivation, weeping eyes, urination, and defecation. Don't administer before reading the label and follow all directions carefully. In addition, many baits (to kill rats, mice, ants, and roach) contain peanut butter and sugar. They smell sweet and taste good, but cause internal bleeding that can be fatal. If you use these baits make sure they are inaccessible to your dog and record the date you put the bait out. Rat poison is rarely fatal as long as you get your dog to the vet as soon as possible.

6

CHOKING

Choking is often caused by bones or rawhide that get stuck in the throat. For example, collies and other long-nosed breeds often get circular marrow bones stuck behind their canine teeth on the lower jaw. A bee sting (see p. 110) in an allergic animal can occasionally lead to choking because it causes a constriction of the throat muscles.

WHAT YOU CAN DO

• Open the dog's mouth. If you can see the lodged object, swipe your fingers across the back of its throat and remove it. This is generally the quickest solution, but being bitten is a risk.

• If you cannot remove the object by hand, try the Heimlich manoeuvre: if your dog is small enough to lift, hold it upright in your arms, wrap your hands directly under its rib cage, and give one forceful squeeze. If your dog is too large to lift or is unconscious, lay it on its side, place both of your hands just behind its bottom rib and press down quickly once or twice.

• As a last resort, try cardiopulmonary resuscitation (CPR) while someone drives you to the veterinary hospital. CPR is normally only used for a dog that isn't breathing and has no pulse. Place your dog on its right side. Remember the "ABCs" of CPR. Airway: open the dog's airway by extending its head and neck, pull its tongue to one side, clear mucus from its nostrils, then use your hand to swipe the back of its throat. Breathing: hold your dog's mouth shut, put your mouth over its nostrils and blow four times. Circulation: place one hand on top of the other with the heel of the bottom hand at the point where your dog's front elbow meets its chest. Press firmly. Perform five compressions, then four breaths. Repeat. Continue CPR until you can detect a strong pulse or until you reach the vet.

• To prevent choking, avoid all bones or rawhide, and be sure chew toys are twice the length as the distance from your dog's chin to the top of its head, so they don't get stuck in its throat.

SYMPTOMS

• Gagging and coughing.
• Pawing at its mouth to try to clear the obstruction.
• Tongue and gums may turn a bluish colour.
• The dog may become unconscious.

6

CONVULSIONS

Convulsions are defined as sudden, uncontrolled busts of activity that last from one to three minutes. Signs of convulsions include salivating and foaming at mouth, and shaking, jerking or stiffening of the legs or entire body. Loss of urine and bowels may also occur. Certain breeds can have hereditary predispositions to diseases that can end up causing convulsions.

CAUSES

- Epilepsy.
- Low blood sugar.
- Poison (for example, antifreeze, chocolate).
- Kidney failure.
- Liver failure.
- Hereditary predisposition.

WHAT YOU CAN DO

- A dog that has had a seizure may appear dazed and unaware of its surroundings, or it may be fine. Never move a dog while it is having a fit and leave it alone until it is over. After this you can put your dog in a calm, quiet, dark room.

- Rub one to two teaspoons of karo syrup or honey onto the gums. This raises the dog's blood sugar instantly.

- Although the average time of a convulsion is only 90 seconds, and your dog may soon appear fine again, always call your vet.

WHAT YOUR VET CAN DO

- Your vet will give the dog a physical examination and take blood and urine tests to try to determine the underlying cause of the convulsions. Recommendations for treatment will be made accordingly (see p. 76).

COMPLEMENTARY TREATMENTS

HOMEOPATHIC REMEDIES
A number of homeopathic treatments can be helpful. These include *Aconitum napellus* 30c, which is valuable in cases where the dog has collapsed because of shock: two pellets under the tongue. Rescue Remedy is good for dogs that are scared or disoriented: two drops every 15 minues for three doses while on the way to the vet.

6

BURNS AND SCALDS

Flames from a house or an outdoor fire are just one type of burn that can affect your dog. A dog's haircoat is extremely flammable and most dogs have not been taught what to do in the event of a fire. This means you need to be especially careful to avoid any situations that may cause burns and scalds.

DANGER ZONES

Apply cool water to minor burns.

• Accidents in the kitchen, especially with new puppies, are not uncommon. Scalding with hot liquids or oils or even touching a hot pan by accident can cause a serious thermal burn. Heating pads used to warm up new litters can cause radiant heat burns that are similar to sunburn.

• Curious puppies chewing on electrical cords can end up with electrical burns that destroy the skin as well as the deeper tissues.

• Smoke inhalation can cause lung damage and respiratory distress that may be apparent immediately, or not until 24 hours later.

• Dogs with severe and extensive burns can go into shock (see p. 109) as a result of the fluid loss and decreased blood flow that occurs through the surface of burned skin.

WHAT YOU AND YOUR VET CAN DO

• For minor burns, cool water soaks with loose-fitting gauze bandages often suffice.

• More severe burns should be addressed by your vet as soon as possible. The prognosis of a burn depends on the percentage of skin affected, the depth and location of the burn, as well as the dog's age and overall health status. Treatment is geared to address shock, replace fluids, maintain breathing, cool the skin and reduce pain. Cleaning the area removes dead tissue and debris. Antibiotics reduce the risk of infection, and proper nutrition counteracts protein and fluid losses. Burns involving more than 50 percent of the skin surface carry a poor prognosis. In many cases euthanasia may be the best solution, as your vet will explain.

Warning

Always contact a vet as soon as possible whenever your pet may have suffered anything other than a minor burn. Many dogs may look fine initially but become distressed within the next 24 hours.

6

HOLIDAY HAZARDS

Taking a few precautions helps ensure a safe, happy holiday season for you and your pets. Dogs get holiday stress just like people. Strangers, unfamiliar decorations, and hectic activity can all take a toll on your dog. Try to maintain routine as much as possible. Regardless of where you go or what you do, be sure you dog has a leash, collar, and proper identification tags.

WHAT YOU CAN DO

• The number-one holiday problem in dogs is indigestion caused by eating too much rich food. Table scraps can cause vomiting, diarrhoea, and put your dog at risk of life-threatening pancreatitis. Don't give your dog bones. They can get stuck in its mouth or perforate its intestines. Plastic wrappers and aluminum foil coated with gravy look good, but can obstruct your dog's intestinal tract. Throw out leftovers and be sure wrappings from food and gifts are properly disposed of. Garbage bins with pet-proof lids are an effective deterrent for hungry hounds. Chocolate, biscuits and sweets can give your dog more than a sour stomach. Chocolate contains theobromide, which is toxic to the nervous system.

• Keep candles elevated, well up out of paws' reach. Tape electrical cords to the floor, use safety-approved lights and unplug them when you're not at home. Frayed light cords can cause shock or burns.

• Not all dogs can swim, so if you go to the seaside take extra care of your pet near water. Get your dog a life jacket for boating and keep the dog on a leash if you are near a jetty where it could slip, or on the beach where it might be washed into the sea by a large wave. Remember too to carry with you something with which to collect your dog's faeces for disposal.

6

CUTS AND BLEEDING

One of the most common accidents a dog can have is a cut or laceration. Bandage material, cleaning material and anticoagulant powder (for nails that have been cut too short) will take care of most minor wounds. Larger wounds should be seen by a vet.

TYPES OF CUTS

• Cuts to the pads of the feet are relatively common. They are often caused by the dog treading on broken glass or a sharp piece of metal that slices through the pad. Although the pad feels much tougher than skin, it does have a large blood supply, with the result that when cut, the paw will bleed profusely.

• Another part of the body that bleeds profusely is the tongue. Dogs are at great risk from such wounds if they are allowed to scavenge, since they frequently lacerate their tongues on the edges of metal cans when attempting to eat any remaining contents. Urgent veterinary attention is needed to stem the blood flow and treat the wound.

• Cuts and lacerations in the mouth often bleed profusely, because of the large blood supply, but they also heal quickly for the same reason. Flush out mouth lesions with a cool solution of salt water (5 ml/1 tsp of salt mixed with 250 ml/8 fl oz of water). Use a turkey baster or large syringe and hold the dog's head down over a bucket. Flush the salt solution into the mouth and let it come out several times. On the first and second day after this feed only broth or purée. By the third day most mouth lesions are healed.

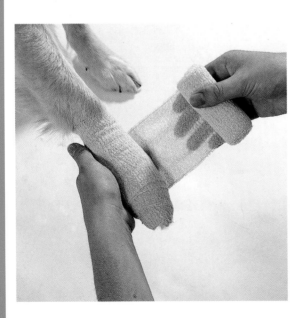

Warning

Be wary of using a tourniquet—if the tie is too tight, it can actually harm the limb, affecting blood circulation to the wound.

Cut foot pads can be cleaned with iodine and peroxide and bandaged.

6

WHAT YOUR VET CAN DO

• If a dog is bleeding, the principle is the same for pets and people. Apply direct pressure to the wound to stop the bleeding. It is best to use gauze or a clean bandage, but anything available—including your hand—will do if necessary. Release the pressure after a couple of minutes.

• If the bleeding stops, access the wound. Use clippers or scissors to remove hair from the area, then take an iodine-type soap and clean up wound. Rinse out again with hydrogen peroxide. If there is lots of hair surrounding the wound, before you clip the hair, coat it with water-soluble KY jelly. The hairs will stick to the jelly and not the wound. Then you will find that they are easy to wash away. Cover the wound with gauze; take it off the next morning and reassess the wound. Give your vet a call if you are at all worried.

• If the bleeding does not stop, continue applying direct pressure to the wound while you're on your way to the vet. For a paw wound, once the dog has been treated by your vet, place a clean sock over the paw to keep the dressing clean, sticking it at the top with tape.

• If you think your dog might bite you because it is hurt, scared, and in pain, protect yourself by using a muzzle. A muzzle can easily be made using a rope or belt, your tie, or even a pair of tights. Drape the material over the dog's nose and under its jaw, criss-cross it and then bring it back behind the head and tie it.

• Homeopathic remedies include *Calendula* 6x: one tablet twice daily until the wound is clearly healing. *Arnica* decreases bruising, while *Hepar sulphuris calcareum* 30c can reduce pain and decrease the risk of swelling and infection in the early stages: one pellet every four hours for three doses.

6

DOG BITES

Over one million people are bitten by dogs each year. This figure probably represents only half the number of actual bites because the rest go unreported. It is thought that 50 percent of children under the age of 12 have been bitten. Any breed of dog has the potential to bite, although some breeds tend to be more aggressive than others because they were bred specifically for the aggressive trait. These dogs are often used to guard, protect, and herd.

WHY DOGS BITE

• Many different things can lead to a dog bite. Sudden movements, such as a child riding a bicycle past a dog, may trigger the dog's hunting instincts causing it to bite.

• The strong bond dogs form with their owners can cause them to become overly protective. Dogs have attacked children in play if one tackles the dog's owner and the dog perceives it as a threat.

• Other dogs become territorial of their garden or house. On walks, a dog may be friendly, but once at home, becomes aggressive to the same people previously tolerated. Some dogs tolerate very little before they become aggressive.

• Some experts think the problem is that dogs do not regard small children as they regard adults. To prevent trouble, dogs should be taught their position at the bottom of the family social ladder. Children should take part in the dog's training and discipline to enforce their authority over the dog.

A muzzle is a sensible way of ensuring your dog cannot bite while in a public place with you.

6

Warning

In many countries there is always a threat of rabies whenever two dogs are involved in a fight with each other. Check with your vet that your dog is up to date on its rabies vaccine and report the incident to your local health authority, as required by law.

WHAT YOU AND YOUR VET CAN DO

• If you are bitten by your dog or someone else's dog, you should seek medical attention. If it is a very superficial wound, clean it really well. Place it under running water for 10 to 15 minutes and clean it with mild soap. Medical attention needs to be sought for any bite or scratch wound that is deep, reddened, swollen, painful or oozing.

• To prevent dog bites, make sure you get obedience training for your dog. Your dog should be willing to please you and consistently respond correctly to commands. Don't use physical punishment for inappropriate behaviour.

• In many cases, neutering the dog or using hormone therapy can suppress aggressive behaviour. At other times, dogs can be simply kept away from situations which cause aggressiveness. Do seek professional advice from your vet if you have any concerns about your dog's behaviour.

COMPLEMENTARY TREATMENTS

□ HOMEOPATHIC REMEDIES
The use of *Hepar sulphuris calcareum* 30c at an early stage will not only relieve the pain, but can also prevent the wound becoming infected. Another remedy which can be used as an alternative is *Arnica montana* 30c, given four times daily.

6

HIT BY CAR

The greatest cause of canine emergencies is road accidents. The term used by vets is "HBC" or "hit by car". Some are fortunate and just have minor wounds, bruises, or lacerations. Most dogs, however, end up with broken bones or suffer other internal injuries. Regardless of how a dog appears to look externally, if it has been hit by a car then it should be examined thoroughly by a vet as soon as possible.

WHAT YOU CAN DO

• The majority of dogs hit by cars are running loose. Keeping your dog on a lead can prevent a lot of unnecessary trauma for pets and owners. Many dogs are run over by their owners as they pull into and out of their driveways. Putting a fenced enclosure or keeping your dog inside helps prevent this.

• Before you try to help an injured dog, be careful because dogs that are severely traumatized are also scared and in pain. Since they usually do not know what is causing the pain, you risk being bitten, even if it is your dog.

• Take a minute to protect yourself by muzzling the dog. You can make a muzzle with a piece of rope, a belt, your tie, or even a pair of tights. Loop the material over and under the dog's nose, then bring the material behind its ears and tie it.

• Injured dogs need to be transported to the vet quickly but calmly. Moving the dog as little as possible is important, especially with certain fractures. You can try lifting a very small dog with your hands, but using a stretcher is generally necessary for large dogs. To make a stretcher, you can use a board or a large blanket. Cover the dog, roll it over onto the blanket, and start sliding it toward the car. Open both doors. The first person should enter backwards, and the second person follows. Close the doors, and off you go. It's also a good idea to call ahead and let your vet know you're on your way.

6

An injured dog will need to be
kept warm. A car blanket or
coat is useful in this instance.

• If your dog is not moving, you need to be sure that it is alive. Touch the
cornea (centre) of its eye. If the dog is alive, it should blink.

• If your dog is unconscious, treat it just like you would treat a person with a
possible spinal injury. Wrap the dog on a board so its legs, spine, and neck are
stiff. Next, be sure that its airway is clear so it is able to breathe. You can
gently extend its head and neck, pull its tongue over to one side of its mouth,
and use a cloth to clear any secretions from its mouth.

• If the dog is bleeding, the first aid treatment, once again, is the same as
used for a person. Apply steady, direct pressure with a clean towel, a piece of
gauze, or even your hand to try to stop or at least limit the blood flow. Two
pellets of *Arnica montana* 20c can be placed on the tongue every 15 minutes
for a total of three doses to relieve pain and decrease swelling while on the
way to the vet.

• Legs that are dangling or obviously broken can be immobilized with splints
made of newspaper, towels, or even a pillow (see p. 104).

WHAT YOUR VET CAN DO

• Once at the hospital, the vet will examine the dog and initially assess vital
statistics including rectal temperature, heart rate, respiration, and gum colour.
If the dog is critical, a catheter or tube will be inserted into a vein, so that
intravenous medication can be given to prevent shock, along with fluids to
stabilize blood pressure. Once the dog is stabilized, X rays will be taken to
detect broken bones and other internal injuries. You will then be advised of
the necessary treatment. You will also be given a prognosis, or told how your
dog should do once out of the hospital, and whether any long-term
complications should be expected.

6

BROKEN BONES

The most common cause of broken bones in dogs is road accidents. Fights between big dogs and little dogs can also result in broken bones. Other causes include falling from a height—such as a table, or the back of a truck—and various bone diseases, including cancer. A dog with a broken leg will hold it in an abnormal position, or you may see that it is at an abnormal angle or very swollen. Open wounds with a piece of bone jutting out are more obvious. Injuries of this type are also at high risk of becoming seriously infected. The dog may let you know it is in pain by limping or being reluctant to put weight on the particular leg, or it might just hold the leg up and not put any weight on it at all. Your dog may not want the leg to be touched, even by you.

WHAT YOU CAN DO

• If you suspect your dog's leg is fractured, immobilizing the leg with a splint helps prevent further injuries, especially if it is a long way to the vet. To make a splint, you can use a few pieces of newspaper, cardboard, or even a soft pillow will work. Wrap them around the fracture and try to include the joint above and below the break, then secure it with tape.

• You can also just tape a bad leg to the good leg. Be careful not to tape it too tightly. This is called a mountaineering splint.

• Moving a dog with a suspected fracture needs to be carried out carefully to avoid worsening the injury. Try to keep the dog as immobile, yet comfortable, as possible on your journey to the vet. This may entail providing support around its body. Place the dog on a flat, firm surface like a board in order to prevent further injuries.

With a simple fracture, the broken limb will be placed in a cast.

6

WHAT YOUR VET CAN DO

• The diagnosis of a fracture is made by taking an X ray of the broken bones. Treatment can consist of using casts, splints, plates, or wires. Casts are made of fibreglass or plaster, but their use is limited. Since the joint above and below a break must be immobilized, a cast cannot be used for fractures involving bones of the hip or shoulder. They work best for simple fractures in the lower part of a leg.

• If a fracture is too complicated to be repaired using a cast, stainless steel pins, wires, and bone plates can be used. Pins or steel rods can be inserted inside broken bones to hold the pieces of bone together. The post-operative care requires limited exercise, to prevent the pins from moving. The rods are left in until the fracture heals—generally four to eight weeks—then removed under local anaesthetic. Orthopaedic wire can be used to put fragments of bone together or to anchor a bone to a pin to make the repair more stable. Stainless steel bone plates are screwed directly into the bone. Plates and screws can be used to repair broken bones with odd shapes, like the pelvis, or badly broken long bones of the front or hind legs. Bone plates are very expensive, but minimal post-operative care is needed.

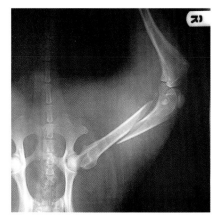 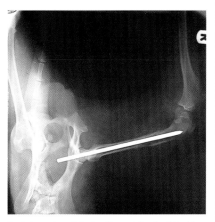

A fracture of the upper bone, or femur, on the hind leg (centre of the picture).

An internal metal pin (the white line) holds the two ends of the broken bone in place.

COMPLEMENTARY TREATMENTS

HOMEOPATHIC REMEDIES
Immediately after the injury has occurred, the use of *Arnica* 30c not only relieves pain, but also helps reduce associated swelling. Give four doses every 15 minutes, until you can get the dog to the vet.

Symphytum 30c will assist the healing of the bone. For older dogs, when healing can be more problematic, *Calcarea fluorica* 30c is also often recommended. Consult your vet regarding the frequency of doses in such cases.

6

WINTERTIME HAZARDS

Winter can present many hazards to dogs. A number of breeds, particularly small ones with short haircoats, have little insulation against the cold. To make enough energy to stay warm, outdoor dogs burn 50 percent more calories in the winter, so their food must be increased accordingly. All dogs are at risk from antifreeze poisoning, which can prove fatal.

FROSTBITE

• Temperatures below –6°C are too cold for most dogs. Cold weather can cause frostbite and hypothermia. The areas most susceptible to frostbite are the extremities.

• Frostbitten tissues turn a greyish-white colour and require gradual rewarming. Don't rub or irritate the areas. Give a lukewarm bath and offer warm fluids (for example, chicken broth).

SYMPTOMS

Frostbite:
• Shivering,
• Pink areas of skin on the extremities lose colour, become red and swollen.

OTHER HAZARDS

• Antifreeze containing ethylene glycol as the active ingredient, is a major wintertime hazard. It has a sweet taste and less than 30 ml (2 tbsp) kills a 4.5-kg dog. Signs include depression, uncoordination, vomiting, and seizures. You must catch this within the first two hours for treatment to be effective. The best type of antifreeze for dog owners contains monopropylene glycol, which is safer for family pets and wildlife, and lasts longer in the car. If you are changing your own antifreeze, be sure to clean up any spills promptly and store the remainder in a sealed container which you can lock away.

• Salt and de-icing chemicals can irritate your dog's feet. Keep a spritzer spray filled with water by your front door to clean your dog's feet when it comes inside. Dry the feet off immediately.

Wrap a dog suffering from hypothermia in a heat-retaining blanket.

6

HEATSTROKE

Heatstroke is caused by a combination of high temperatures, humidity, dehydration and poor ventilation. It is a major danger for dogs. In spite of warnings from animal-welfare organizations, it is a sad fact that many dogs die from heatstroke after being left in unattended vehicles on hot summer days.

WHAT YOU CAN DO

• Never leave your dog in a parked car, as the temperature in it can reach 49°C (120°F) or higher in less than 30 minutes when the outdoor temperature is 30°C (86°F). Dogs do not perspire like people do; they pant to cool down. Therefore, they are very susceptible to heatstroke. Breeds with pushed-in faces (like Pekingese or pugs), the very young, and the elderly are at greatest risk.

SYMPTOMS

• Restlessness and visible distress.
• Excessive panting.
• Drooling.
• Unsteadiness on feet.
• Bright red gums.

• Rapid action is needed to save the life of a dog suffering from heatstroke. Permanent brain damage can occur when the body temperature reaches or exceeds 41°C (105.8°F). If untreated, heatstroke can lead to kidney failure. Coma and death can result in severe cases.

• To cool your dog down, bring it inside, give it a cool bath, spray it with a hose, or pour alcohol down its back. Offer it cool fluids. Take its temperature (normal is 38–39°C/100.4–102°F) with a rectal thermometer. You should monitor the dog's temperature about every 10 minutes and remove it from the water once it falls back to the normal level. If you are worried or don't have a thermometer, call your vet. In extreme cases, a vet may need to administer subcutaneous fluids as well as medication to decrease the body temperature. Give your dog Rescue Remedy (three drops every 15 minutes) while on your way to the vet.

COMPLEMENTARY TREATMENTS

☐ HOMEOPATHIC REMEDIES
Glonoine 30c can help to bring relief in cases of heatstroke (two pellets while on the way to the vet).

EMERGENCIES

In spite of all best efforts, emergencies do happen. You should know your vet's procedures for emergency situations, especially the ones that occur outside opening hours. Being able to recognize a true emergency allows you to react more appropriately in a stressful situation. Keep the telephone number of your vet, as well as that of a local emergency facility, in a convenient place.

EMERGENCY SITUATIONS

• Pet poisoning is a major problem. Three of the most common types of poisoning are antifreeze, rodenticide, and eating rubbish. Anytime you suspect a poisoning, call your vet as soon as possible. Symptoms of some poisons do not become apparent until 24 to 72 hours after the fact. In the case of antifreeze, the first few hours are critical. After that, most dogs die because of irreversible kidney damage regardless of therapy.

• In addition to poisoning, other conditions that usually require emergency care include road accidents, suspected broken bones, severe bleeding, eye injuries, difficulty in breathing, collapse or convulsions (seizures), inability to urinate, choking, vomiting and/or diarrhoea for over 24 hours, appetite loss for over two days in a row, severe depression, bloated stomach, or rectal temperature under 36°C (96.8°F) or over 40°C (104°F).

SYMPTOMS

Poisoning:
• Vomiting and diarrhoea in the case of ingestion,
• Swelling or burning on the skin, if poison is spilt on to the skin and coat,
• In severe cases, fits and eventual collapse.

FIRST AID KIT

Keeping a first aid kit on hand for emergencies can be helpful for minor cuts and wounds, as well as accidental poisonings. In addition to the standard items in any first aid kit, include:

• Hydrogen peroxide (3%) (works well to induce vomiting, but first talk to your vet to determine when you do or do not want to induce vomiting); Pepto Bismol (for an upset stomach); Kaopectate tablets (for diarrhoea); generic Benadryl capsules (for allergic reactions); saline eye drops (to flush out eye contaminants); and artificial tear ointment (to lubricate eyes after flushing).

• Other useful items include a rectal thermometer, a turkey baster or bulb syringe (good for giving certain medications by mouth or to flush wounds), white petroleum jelly, bandage scissors, gauze sponges and bandages, a self-adhering athletic bandage, tweezers (to remove stings), and rubbing alcohol.

• Dishwashing liquid (with a mild grease-cutting action) can be used to bathe the dog after skin contamination to reduce exposure (to insecticides, for example). Rubber gloves will protect you while bathing your dog.

6

SHOCK

• Being able to recognize signs of shock can help save lives. Shock is defined as a collapse of the cardiovascular system (heart, lungs, blood circulation). It is a group of signs that occurs as a result of a life-threatening disease process or situation. There are different types of shock, and each type can be associated with an emergency.

• Signs of shock include bright red gums initially, later they are a pale white colour; rapid heartbeat; collapse; shivering; cold extremities; and weak pulse. Severe shock will lead to irreversible damage and death unless treated promptly. Treatment consists of intravenous fluids and steroids, warming to raise body temperature, and therapy for the underlying disease or condition.

• In an emergency, you can first evaluate your dog's condition by taking the dog's temperature (normal is 38–39°C); taking the pulse (heart) rate (normal heart rates are 110–120 beats per minute for puppies, 80–120 for small-breed adult dogs, and 60–80 for large-breed adult dogs); and measuring the rate of respiration (normal is 20–22 breaths per minute in a young dog, and 14–16 in an adult dog). Check gums for colour and how long it takes for them to return to normal when you press on them with your index finger for one second and release. (The gum colour should return to a bright pink in one to three seconds). You should know how to put on a muzzle and have one at hand. You should also be able to perform CPR (see p. 94) and check for eye responses (see p. 102) to see whether the animal is actually alive.

> ## Tip
>
> When you contact your vet or the emergency facility, be ready to provide the following information: your name, address, and telephone number; information about any poison (amount eaten, time since the exposure occurred, exact type of poison involved) or problem; the breed, age, sex, and weight of the dog or dogs involved; the current status of the animal.

Poisonous algae grow on stagnant water at certain times of the year. If your dog jumps in and swallows any of the water while swimming, it may be poisoned.

6

STINGS AND BITES

Young dogs are particularly vulnerable to stings or bites because of their youthful curiosity. They occur in different places. If the dog attempts to eat an insect, it will be stung in the back of the mouth. If on the dog's coat you may not be able to see a sting or bite, in which case you will have to rely on your dog's reactions for diagnosis.

WHAT YOU CAN DO

• Bee stings are a frequent problem in dogs, especially those who stick their noses in the wrong spot. The most common sign is a big swollen muzzle. You can make a thick paste from bicarbonate of soda and water and put it on the sting. This is very soothing because it helps neutralize the acid venom. If you have Benadryl on hand then call your vet for proper dose. This antihistamine helps decrease the swelling. You can also rub one drop of nettle extract directly on the sting. Most dogs will be fine, but occasionally some dogs have breathing difficulties and need to be watched carefully for 24 hours.

• In areas where there are snakes it is useful to have a snake-bite kit. Find the kind that uses suction to remove the venom. If your dog does get bitten by a snake, compress the wound and the area above the wound, carefully pick up your dog, and take it to a vet for a shot of anti-venom. You must try to keep the dog as still as possible because movement increases the circulation, which increases the rate at which the venom moves into the dog's body. Don't put ice on the wound either for the same reason.

SYMPTOMS

• Swelling around the mouth and throat may occur if your dog has been stung there by a wasp or a bee.
• If your dog has been bitten by a snake, it may begin to tremble, drool or vomit, and may collapse.

6

USEFUL ADDRESSES

BRITISH HOLISTIC VETERINARY MEDICAL
ASSOCIATION
Mrs Sue Thomas
The Croft,
Tockwith Road,
Longmarston,
Yorks YO26 7PQ
Association of qualified veterinary
practitioners with skills in
complementary therapies. Write for
details of practitioners in your area.

BRITISH HOMEOPATHIC ASSOCIATION
27a Devonshire Street,
London W1N 1RJ
tel: 0207 935 2163
Can provide a list of medically
qualified homeopathic vets.

ROYAL COLLEGE OF VETERINARY
SURGEONS
62–64 Horseferry Road,
London SW1P 2AF
tel: 0207 222 2001
fax: 0207 222 2004
http://www.rcvs.org.uk/rcvs/
UK statutory body for the veterinary
profession. Can provide a list of
veterinary surgeons in your area.
Information about pet problems may
be obtained from the website.

ALTERNATIVE VETERINARY MEDICINE
CENTRE
Chinham House
Stanford in the Vale
Faringdon
Oxon SN7 8NQ
Write to the Hon.Sec. for a list of those
alternative medical practitioners
specializing in holistic treatment in
your area.

NATIONAL CANINE DEFENCE LEAGUE
17 Wakley Street,
London EC1V 7RQ
tel: 0171 837 0006
Registered charity which is concerned
with protecting and defending all dogs
from any form of mistreatment.

BLUE CROSS
Field Centre, Shilton Road,
Burford,
Oxford 0X18 4PF
tel: 01993 822651
fax: 01993 823 083
Animal charity which relies on
donations to provide free veterinary
care for animals in low-income
families. Has adoption centres for
animals needing new homes.

ASSOCIATION OF PET DOG TRAINERS
Peacocks Farm,
Northchapel,
Petworth,
West Sussex GU28 9JD
enquiry line: 01428 707 234
Ensures members use fair and kind
methods when training dogs. Has a
directory of assessed trainers.

WWW HOMEPAGES
http://www.altvetmed.com
AltVetMed – general alternative medicine

http://www.naturalholistic.com
Natural Holistic Pet Care – general
alternative medicine

http://home.earthlink.net/~fourwinds
Four Winds Holistic Animal Services –
general alternative medicine

http://www.med.auth.gr/~karanik/engli
sh/vetr.htm
The Veterinary Acupuncture Page

6

INDEX

ACKNOWLEDGMENTS
t = top; b = bottom; c = centre; l = left; r = right
1-5, 9, 25, 26, 41, 43l, 45, 48, 53t, 54, 63, 68, 79, 89, 94, 96, 98 David King; 6, 42 Christine Steimer/ Oxford Scientific Films; 7 David Jordan; 8r, l, 17, 18b, 24b, 27t, b, 29b, 30b, 31, 33b, 35b, 39b, 43tr, cr, br, 47b, 51, 52, 53b, 55t, b, 58b, 61, 69, 73b, 76, 81, 88, 107b Andrew Sydenham; 10, 57 Adriano Bacchella/Bruce Coleman; 11, 23, 58t , 60, 95, 102, 104 Sally Anne Thompson/Animal Photography; 12, 14, 15, 16, 32, 46b, 49, 64, 71, 78b, 86, 92, 100, 103, 105l, r, 106 Jane Burton; 18t Stephen Oliver/ RSPCA Photolibrary; 19, 50t, 65, John Daniels; 20, 30t J-L Klein & M-L Hubert/Oxford Scientific Films; 21 E. A. Janes/RSPCA Photolibrary; 22 David Barron/Oxford Scientific Films; J. B. Blossom/RSPCA Photolibrary; 29t, 37, 56, 73t, 77, 80, 87, 101, 109, 110 Jane Burton/ Warren Photographic; 35t, 36, 83, 91, 99 John Daniels/Ardea; 38t, 60 (inset) Bradley Viner; 38b Nobert Lange/Oxford Scientific Films; 44t John Clegg/Ardea; 44b, 74, 93 Jane Burton/ Bruce Coleman; 46t Dr Gary Gaugler/Oxford Scientific Films; 47t M. Watson/Ardea; 50b Hans Reinhard/Bruce Coleman; 59, 62, 82, 97 Angela Hampton/ RSPCA Photolibrary; 78t Tim Sambrook/RSPCA Photolibrary; 84 Kim Taylor/Bruce Coleman; 90t R. Willbie/ Animal Photography; 107t Cheryl A. Ertelt/RSPCA Photolibrary